W9-DBD-268

IN MEMORY

OF

SPENCER SOMMERS BLATZ

1 9 4 2 -- 1 9 6 4

DONATED BY

SECURITY CREDIT

Its Economic Role and Regulation

HG6041
B6

SECURITY CREDIT

Its Economic Role and Regulation

Jules I. Bogen

Professor of Finance

and

Herman E. Krooss

Professor of Economics

GRADUATE SCHOOL OF BUSINESS ADMINISTRATION
NEW YORK UNIVERSITY

Englewood Cliffs, N.J.

PRENTICE-HALL, INC.

NO LONGER THE PROPERTY

OF THE

UNIVERSITY OF R.I. LIBRARY

© 1960, BY

NEW YORK STOCK EXCHANGE

ALL RIGHTS RESERVED. NO PART OF THIS BOOK
MAY BE REPRODUCED IN ANY FORM, BY MIMEO-
GRAPH OR ANY OTHER MEANS, WITHOUT PER-
MISSION IN WRITING FROM THE AUTHOR.

LIBRARY OF CONGRESS
CATALOG CARD NUMBER: 60-16627

PRINTED IN THE UNITED STATES OF AMERICA

79900 — MO

PREFACE

Economic growth requires the raising of huge amounts of capital to finance the expansion of output of goods and services.

Under a free enterprise system, capital is raised externally by business concerns from individuals who have savings available for investment and the institutions to which individuals entrust their savings. In a Communist society, by contrast, the State owns all business and capital is provided exclusively by organs of the Government.

The raising of funds to finance expansion of a free enterprise economy is vastly facilitated by an active capital market. Such a market performs two basic, closely-related functions. By bringing together the enterprises that require capital and the individuals and institutions that have savings to invest, new capital formation is facilitated. Equally important, the capital market enables owners of outstanding securities to sell them to others when they want cash. It is only because securities are readily marketable that individual and institutional investors are willing to invest freely in stocks and bonds, since otherwise funds so invested would become frozen for long periods of time or indefinitely. The quality of marketability imparted to publicly-owned stocks by an active securities market also explains why stockholders are content to have so large a part of current earnings retained and reinvested by corporations rather than distributed as cash dividends, since such reinvestment tends to be reflected in market price appreciation.

The use of credit is essential to the functioning of the capital market, as to other sectors of the economy. Underwriters and distributors of securities, like other merchants that carry inventories, must borrow freely to finance their operations. Investors and traders find it desirable from time to time to use borrowed funds to supplement their own resources in purchasing and holding securities. Brokers and dealers borrow to finance their own and their customers' transactions.

Despite the key role of the capital market in the functioning of our economy and the major importance of security loans to the operation of the capital market, economic literature contains surprisingly few studies of this subject. A large part of the existing literature is polemic or apologetic, attacking or defending the use of credit in the stock market rather than investigating objectively its role in the economy.

The Securities Exchange Act of 1934 provided for qualitative control of security loans by the Board of Governors of the Federal Reserve System for the first time. Completion of a quarter of a century of experience with such regulation makes a comprehensive and objective study of the role of credit in the security markets timely.

This study has been planned and conducted by Dr. Jules I. Bogen, Professor of Finance, and Dr. Herman E. Krooss, Professor of Economics in the Graduate School of Business Administration of New York University. Invaluable assistance in providing statistical and other data has been received from the New York Stock Exchange, the Federal Reserve Bank of New York and the Department of Banking of the State of New York. The authors are solely responsible, however, for the conclusions reached.

The Graduate School is particularly indebted to Jonathan A. Brown, Director, and Stan West, Associate Director, of the Department of Research & Statistics of the New York Stock Exchange for their counsel and readiness to make available results of their extensive pioneering studies in this field.

The Graduate School of Business Administration received a grant from the New York Stock Exchange to finance this research project. This assistance is gratefully acknowledged.

September 1, 1960   JOSEPH H. TAGGART
                                         Dean, Graduate School of
                                         Business Administration
                                         New York University

CONTENTS

vii

LIST OF TABLES AND CHARTS

CHARTS   Page

SECURITY CREDIT

Its Economic Role and Regulation

Chapter 1

HISTORY OF SECURITY CREDIT BEFORE 1934

Credit, the use of promises to pay money, has performed an essential role in economic life since ancient times.

Modern economies are characterized by the ubiquitous use of credit on a vast and expanding scale. Businesses and farmers, small and large, buy goods on credit and borrow money to finance their activities and needs for productive facilities, inventories and other assets. Governments—national, state and local—borrow huge sums for public works, defense and other purposes. Individuals, rich and poor, use credit to finance purchases of homes, automobiles, education of children and manifold other needs.

One form of credit that has assumed importance in the modern economy has been security loans; i.e., loans secured by stocks and bonds as collateral. Security loans have been made by banks ever since governments and corporations have issued securities publicly. In England, mention is found of loans secured by shares of the early joint stock companies in the seventeenth and early eighteenth centuries. Bankers and other lenders have consistently sought the added protection provided by the pledge, as collateral, of securities for which a constant and ready market is available.

Security collateral loans, known as Lombard loans, have long been utilized in Europe. But it is in the United States that security loans have performed their greatest role in helping to promote economic and financial development.

Security Loans Before 1913

Banks began making loans against the pledge of Government bonds as collateral soon after United States bonds were first issued

1

under Hamilton's funding plan of 1791. Thus, even before 1800, loans secured by Government obligations helped provide credit for the commercial needs of the infant economy.[1]

In financing the War of 1812, the Treasury relied heavily upon sales of its bonds in large blocks to wealthy investors. These purchasers obtained cash to pay for the bonds in considerable part by pledging these bonds as collateral for loans from banks.

Loans secured by stocks and bonds became a really important bank asset in this country during the era of internal improvements that followed the War of 1812. Bonds of turnpikes, canals, railroads and land companies generally could be sold in the embryonic capital market of the new nation, with its meager savings and financial resources, only because buyers could borrow the requisite funds from their banks with the securities pledged as collateral. Even many newly organized banks in the pre-Civil War era could find buyers for their shares only by lending the needed funds to subscribers with the stock pledged as collateral.

Since many purchasers of securities had to borrow money to complete payment, brokers early undertook the functions of providing credit on purchased securities pledged as collateral or arranging for such credit at banks.

A financial development of the greatest significance for banking and for the American economy in the third and fourth decades of the nineteenth century was the evolution of a market for call loans in New York City.[2] These are loans secured by stocks and bonds, repayable at the option of either lender or borrower on demand. Because of the existence of a unit banking system, commercial banks throughout the country kept balances in New York. The New York City banks holding these balances, which were subject to sudden withdrawal at any time, required a high degree of liquidity. In the absence of short-term Treasury securities or a well-developed bill market like that of London, call loans on stock exchange collateral provided the favored liquidity medium.

---

[1] N. S. B. Gras, *The Massachusetts First National Bank of Boston, 1784-1934* (Cambridge: Harvard University Press, 1937), pp. 48-51.

[2] Margaret G. Myers, *The New York Money Market* (New York: Columbia University Press, 1931), Vol. I, especially Chap. VII, "The Origin of the Call Loan Market."

"Prior to the institution of the Federal Reserve System," a survey of the call money market published in the *Federal Reserve Bulletin* of April, 1920, states, "bankers, especially in reserve centers, were accustomed to look upon call loans as their principal secondary reserve on the theory that, inasmuch as these loans were payable upon demand, funds so invested could always be promptly obtained on short notice."

The annual reports by national banks to the Comptroller of the Currency show that call loans on stock and bond collateral comprised about a third of all loans by national banks in New York City in the 1870's, and nearly one-half by the opening years of the twentieth century. The growth of such lending by national banks is shown in Chart I. As the earliest available series of security loan statistics, these figures show the almost continuous expansion of such loans by national banks to meet the growing demand for security credit between 1881 and 1920. Moreover, as state banks and trust companies grew in importance during this period, national banks accounted for a declining proportion of total commercial bank lending on securities.

New York banks were the chief, but by no means the only, lenders on security collateral in the latter part of the nineteenth century. The records show that out-of-town banks, savings banks, insurance companies, merchants and wealthy individuals offered to lend funds to brokers on stock market collateral, particularly during periods of credit ease.

Benefits to Economy

The ready availability of relatively large amounts of bank funds for lending on stock exchange collateral had a number of far-reaching economic results. It made possible the distribution of stocks of railroads and other large enterprises to American investors and speculators, so that control of our industries was not acquired by investors in England and other European countries as was the case with enterprises in other Western Hemisphere countries. With most of the equity capital provided at home, foreign capital could be raised for American enterprises chiefly through the sale in European markets of bonds that gave no voting power or share in profits.

A second result was the provision of liquidity to the commercial banking system under normal conditions. In the absence of a call money market, the New York banks would have been under pressure to acquire less liquid and lower quality assets with the funds deposited with them by out-of-town banks, which would have undermined their financial strength.

A third consequence was the adoption by American stock exchanges of the practice of daily cash settlements of transactions. In the early history of the New York Stock Exchange, deliveries were delayed up to 60 days to give time to the buyers to make payment. The ready availability of call money permitted immediate cash payment, so that daily settlements of stock exchange transactions became usual after 1857.[3] Other financial centers, like London and Paris, not having a well-developed call money market, adopted a system of fortnightly settlements, which involved considerably greater risk of insolvency of exchange members.

Most important of all the consequences of the development of a large call money market in New York, needless to say, was the broadening of the market for security issues to provide the long-term capital needed to finance economic growth.[4]

Periods of Credit Stringency

Although the call money market played a vital and constructive role in American economic development during this era of rapid growth, it was subject to occasional periods of strain that attracted public criticism and deeply affected the public's attitude toward the use of security credit.

The supply of call loans on stock exchange collateral, just because such loans were the chief liquidity medium of the banking system, proved highly sensitive to occasional concerted with-

---

[3] For reasons of record-keeping convenience rather than to defer cash payment, the New York Stock Exchange permitted 2 days for delivery and payment from 1933 to 1946; 3 days from 1946 to 1952, and 4 days since 1952.

[4] H. Parker Willis and Jules I. Bogen, *Investment Banking* (New York: Harper & Brothers, 1936), pp. 220-21.

Chart I

SECURITY LOANS BY NATIONAL BANKS *

1881–1920

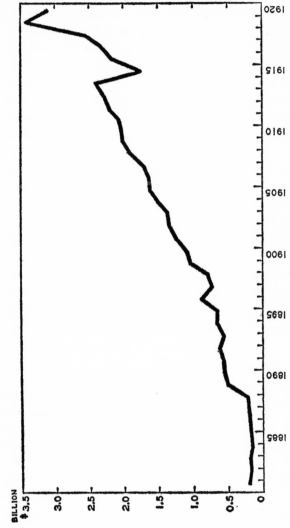

* For all years, demand loans secured by stocks and bonds. 1915-1920: includes time loans; 1889-1914: includes time loans and loans secured by real estate security. Figures include Alaska, Hawaii, and Virgin Islands.

SOURCE: *Annual Reports of the Comptroller of the Currency.*

drawals of funds by banks throughout the country from their New York correspondents. Borrowers were then called upon to repay their security loans on a large scale at the very time when offerings of such funds were quite scarce or non-existent. The result necessarily was heavy forced selling of securities and a rise in call loan rates for a few days to fantastic levels, as high as 5% a month in the panic of 1857, up to 1½% a day in the panic of 1873, and 3% per day in the panic of 1884.

Such high interest rates, prevailing only for very brief periods, were a symptom rather than a cause of the financial panics of these years. The immediate cause of the panics was the general rush for cash that compelled banks throughout the country to draw balances from the financial center, in order to pay out funds being withdrawn by their own depositors.

Experiences during financial panics demonstrated that call loans on stock exchange collateral, despite their high quality, were not always a suitable ultimate source of liquidity for the banking system. One major reason for the establishment of the Federal Reserve System in 1913 was to mobilize the bank reserves of the country in 12 Federal Reserve banks, to provide a reservoir of funds that could be drawn upon to furnish liquidity to banks where and when needed. The liquidity offered by the Federal Reserve banks was expected to curtail the role both of interbank deposits and security loans.

Security Loans During the World War I Period

Establishment of the Federal Reserve System, contrary to the expectations of its founders, curtailed the volume neither of security loans nor of interbank deposits. Actually, the opposite proved to be the case. Economic and financial developments favoring a wider use of security credit proved far more effective in determining the trend of such loans than the shift of legal reserve balances of member banks from their New York correspondents into the Federal Reserve banks.

During the years preceding World War I, according to a survey of the New York call money market by the Federal Reserve Bank of New York, "the volume of all money, both time and call, employed in the securities market was estimated at about

$1,000,000,000, of which the average on call was about 60% and
the average on time about 40%, or a normal volume of call money,
say, of $600,000,000." [5]

In the World War I period, a major expansion of loans secured
by U. S. Government obligations facilitated financing by the
Treasury. At the same time, economic expansion and rising security markets increased the volume of collateral loans on other
classes of securities. Reporting member banks of the Federal
Reserve System at the end of 1919 had outstanding over $1
billion of loans secured by U. S. Government obligations and
over $3 billion of loans secured by other stocks and bonds. These
totals indicate that a severalfold increase in security loans occurred between 1914 and 1919, the first five years of operation
of the Federal Reserve System.

The Decade of the 1920's

Security loans underwent their greatest expansion during the
1920's.

Economic conditions during this decade were highly propitious
for the expanded use of security credit. Rising profits and dividends made common stocks quite attractive and caused share
prices to advance persistently and often sharply. Expanding personal incomes and savings broadened interest in equity investment. Confidence that the nation was embarked upon a "new
era" of uninterrupted economic growth encouraged the purchase
of securities with borrowed money on an unprecedented scale.

Chart II shows how borrowing by members of the New York
Stock Exchange increased with the rise in the level of stock
prices.

At the end of October, 1929, when the boom reached its
culmination, upwards of $17 billion of security collateral loans
of all types made to all classes of borrowers were outstanding,
according to estimates prepared for Senator Carter Glass. These
loans were divided as follows: [6]

---

[5] *Federal Reserve Bulletin*, April, 1920.

[6] Operation of the National and Federal Reserve Banking Systems, *Hearings before a Sub-Committee of the Committee on Banking and Currency*, U. S. Senate,
Appendix, Pt. VII, 1931. This inclusive computation includes all bank security
loans, as well as loans to brokers and dealers from non-bank sources.

Bank loans to brokers and dealers .... $ 2,824,000,000
Loans to brokers and dealers by others   6,416,000,000
Bank security loans to other customers   7,875,000,000
                                                 ─────────────
        Total $17,115,000,000

The experiences of the 1920's demonstrated that:

1. High interest rates on security loans can bring forth a great expansion in the supply of such funds made available to lenders, at a rate that may greatly outpace the growth of the economy.

2. Efforts by the Federal Reserve authorities to discourage expansion of loans to brokers by member banks through public statements and "moral suasion" in 1928 and 1929 were effective, so that security loans by these banks remained relatively static during this period. But this restraint on the part of member banks was more than offset by a very large expansion of loans to brokers by non-bank or "other" lenders, including business corporations, foreign banks and individuals, who were attracted by the high rates available on call loans. Moreover, the New York banks felt they could not refuse to place loans to brokers for customers who wished to make such loans, since there was no statutory bar at the time to the performance of this service.

3. When the public demand for security credit becomes strong enough because of widespread confidence that securities will rise in price, and the supply of funds from the usual sources is restricted, borrowers seek to obtain funds through other channels.[7]

Loans to brokers and dealers "for the account of others," arranged largely through New York banks, increased from $3.7 billion to $6.4 billion between October, 1928 and October, 1929. The Federal Reserve authorities were powerless at that time to curtail such lending, and the New York banks through which most such loans were arranged felt they were not in a position to refuse to perform a service that others were quite ready to undertake in any event. Thus, limitation on lending by banks merely stimulated the placing of loans by other lenders who were eager to take advantage of call money rates that reached a high of 20% per annum in April, 1929.

─────────

[7] For present-day counterparts of this tendency, see Chap. XI.

Chart II
NEW YORK STOCK EXCHANGE MEMBER BORROWINGS *
AND TREND OF STOCK PRICES †
1919–1929

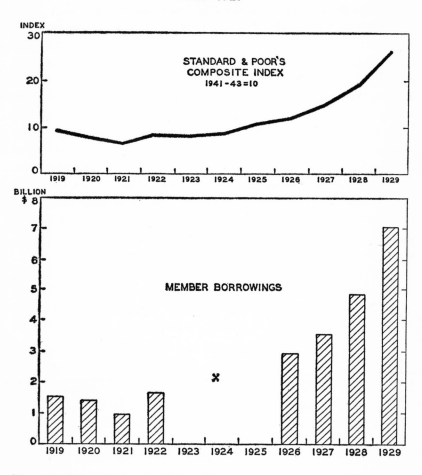

* June 30; † June Average. ✕ Not available.
SOURCE: New York Stock Exchange; Standard & Poor's.

Depression Consequences

The drastic decline in security prices that accompanied the severe depression of the early 1930's necessitated wholesale liquidation of security loans. Forced selling to meet margin calls, in turn, intensified the decline in security prices. A cycle of margin calls, forced sales, price declines and new margin calls characterized much of the period from October, 1929, to the middle of 1932.

A number of causes brought about the depression of the early 1930's, in many respects the most severe in American economic history. The bank failure epidemic, the world-wide decline in commodity prices and international trade, wholesale foreclosures of short-term non-amortized real estate mortgages, drastic deflation of farm income—these were both consequences and contributing causes of the depression.

The decline in borrowings by members of the New York Stock Exchange from $8.5 billion in September, 1929, to $380 million in September, 1932, played a similar dual role. The persistent pressure to repay security loans, which was a consequence of the decline in security prices brought on by the depression, curtailed spending by those affected and so contributed to the downward trend in business and commodity prices.

Bank loans on securities to customers other than brokers and dealers underwent a corresponding contraction.

These depression experiences led to inauguration of regulation of security credit by the Federal Reserve authorities under the Securities Exchange Act of 1934. Before considering the evolution of security credit regulation and its consequences during the past 25 years, security lending will be analyzed in the chapters immediately following from the viewpoints of borrowers, lenders, the economy as a whole and the problem of credit control.

SUMMARY

Security lending in the United States began before 1800 and developed during the era of internal improvements following the War of 1812. Such loans assumed major importance in New

York, as brokers' loans became the chief source of liquidity for the banks in the nation's financial center.

The availability of security credit helped to keep control of railroads and other large enterprises within the country, to provide liquidity for the banking system and, after 1857, to make possible cash settlement of transactions on the New York and other stock exchanges. However, periodic money panics, when concerted calling of loans resulted in very high rates of interest for call money for brief periods, were a factor leading to establishment of the Federal Reserve System.

It was assumed that security lending would dwindle in volume and importance under the Federal Reserve System.

Contrary to these expectations, security credit underwent its greatest expansion after 1913, and especially during the 1920's. The depression of the early 1930's was accompanied by a drastic liquidation of security loans which was caused by but also contributed to the economic contraction of the time.

Chapter 2

PURPOSES OF SECURITY LOANS

Collateral or Purpose

The term "security loans" may refer either to the *character of collateral* pledged to secure loans or to the *purpose* for which loans are incurred by the borrowers.

In the first sense, security loans include all advances *secured by the pledge of stocks and bonds as collateral.* The fact that a loan is thus secured may or may not be related to the purpose for which the borrower incurs the loan. Loans secured by stocks and bonds may be made for as many different purposes, in fact, as are unsecured loans.

Reasons why stocks and bonds are pledged as security for loans, regardless of their purpose, are:

1. To induce the lender to make a loan that he would not be willing to make without the protection of the collateral.

2. To cause the lender to advance a larger sum than he would be willing to lend without the collateral.

3. To obtain a loan at a lower rate of interest than would have to be paid if securities were not pledged to protect the lender.

In its second sense, the term "security loan" describes loans incurred *for the purpose of purchasing or carrying securities.* This is the usual sense in which the term is now employed, both in the security business and in banking statistics. Regulation of security credit applies only to such loans. While the great bulk of loans made for this purpose are secured by stocks and bonds as collateral, unsecured business or personal loans also may be used by borrowers to obtain funds for purchasing or carrying securities.

Credit extended by stock exchange firms to margin account customers is almost exclusively for the purpose of purchasing or carrying securities. Even in such cases, however, a customer may withdraw cash for other purposes and thereby increase his indebtedness to the firm.

This chapter considers the purposes for which all loans secured by stock and bond collateral are incurred.

Major Classifications by Reason

There are four major classes into which loans secured by stocks and bonds as collateral can be grouped, according to the reason for which they are incurred. These are:

1. Loans to purchase or carry securities for investment and speculation.

2. Loans to finance the business of originating, distributing and trading in securities.

3. Loans incurred for other business needs.

4. Loans to finance consumption and other personal credit requirements.

Comprehensive statistics of security collateral loans classified according to purpose are not available. Lenders are not ordinarily concerned with the purpose for which such loans are made where the collateral assures them ample protection. However, regulation of security credit since 1934 has made it necessary for banks to inquire whether loans for which stocks are pledged as collateral are for some purpose other than purchasing or carrying registered securities.

Loans to Purchase or Carry Securities

Loans for "purchasing or carrying securities" are the only classification of bank loans with stocks and bonds pledged as collateral for which regular statistics are published. At the end of June, 1959, the commercial banks of the country had an estimated $2,320 million of such loans outstanding to brokers and dealers, and $1,940 million to other borrowers. In addition, according to a study by the Department of Research and Statistics of the New York Stock Exchange, all brokers and dealers in the United States were borrowing $850 million on that date from United States agencies of foreign banks and $1,070 million from other sources, chiefly through repurchase agreements with corporations covering U. S. Government securities.

The total of $6,180 million measures far more than the volume of loans made by commercial banks and others for "purchasing or carrying securities" for investment or speculation by individuals. The statistics also include all bank loans to security brokers and dealers, and so include loans used to finance security underwriting and distribution, as well as dealer inventories. The Department of Research and Statistics of the New York Stock Exchange estimated that all security brokers and dealers were using $2,690 million on June 30, 1959 to finance underwritings and inventories, including large dealer inventories of U. S. Government securities. Some part of broker borrowings, moreover, doubtless resulted from withdrawals from customer accounts of funds that were to be used for business or consumption purposes.

It is also true that the reported total of loans to borrowers other than brokers and dealers "for purchasing or carrying securities" may not include all loans made by banks for such purpose, particularly at times when high margin requirements prevail. Included under this heading are all loans on stocks subject to Regulation U of the Board of Governors of the Federal Reserve System, regardless of purpose. For other loans, however, the current instructions issued to member banks specify:

> For the purpose of the condition report, the determination whether or not a given secured or unsecured loan was made for the purpose of purchasing or carrying stocks or other securities may be made on the basis of such information as the reporting bank has available. If information is not available as to the purpose of a loan secured by stocks and bonds, the loan may be presumed to be:
> (1) "commercial and industrial" if the borrower is a business enterprise;
> (2) "other loans to farmers" if the borrower is a farmer; and
> (3) for the purpose of purchasing or carrying securities if the borrower is not a business enterprise, a farmer, or a bank.

Under these instructions, considerable diversity of practice developed among banks during the 1940's and 1950's in classifying security loans to others than brokers and dealers. It was believed that some loans that were probably made for the purpose of purchasing and carrying securities were reported as commercial loans.

To provide a closer check on bank loans made to finance security purchases, Regulation U was amended, effective June 15, 1959. The changed provisions required that a statement from the borrower which states merely what is not the purpose of a loan shall be supported by a notation by the bank lending officer describing what is the purpose. The Board of Governors of the Federal Reserve System has never required a sworn statement of the purpose of security loans, however.

Investment and Speculative Objectives

Persons who borrow money to help pay for securities they acquire for investment or speculation may have one or more of several objectives in view.

It is sometimes assumed that their objective is solely to carry securities with borrowed money for a rise in price that will permit them to realize capital gains. But money is borrowed by investors or speculators also:

1. To profit from an excess of current yield on securities over the cost of money borrowed to pay for them. When the interest cost of borrowing is substantially below available yields, investors can profit from "the carry." Large amounts of higher-yielding bonds and other securities have been carried with borrowed money with this end in view.

2. To finance privileged subscriptions to new offerings of stock or convertible bonds offered by a corporation to its stockholders. Often, stockholders do not have funds immediately available to exercise rights they receive to a new offering, but will exercise the rights with borrowed money and then pay off the loan as occasion permits. Borrowing for this objective greatly facilitates the raising of new equity capital by corporations from their shareowners.

3. To pay for stock purchasable under restricted stock pur-

chase options or other employee stock purchase plans. Since stock
so acquired must ordinarily be held for a specified period, credit
is frequently required to finance the transaction.

4. To anticipate the investment of future income. Such income
as received will be used to repay the sums borrowed on securities.
In effect, this kind of borrowing permits the purchase of securities for investment on an instalment basis. Borrowing for this
objective is more common at times when bargain investment opportunities in securities are believed to be available.

Some have questioned whether the purchase of securities with
borrowed money can be considered investment, rather than
speculation. The answer to such questions involves clarification
of the distinction between investment and speculation.

Distinction Between Investment and Speculation

From the viewpoint of the economy as a whole, investment and
speculation are identical in most respects. Both are a part of the
process of capital formation by which savings are invested pro-
ductively.

The distinction arises from the viewpoint of the person who
commits his funds. The investor seeks to minimize the risks he
assumes. The speculator willingly incurs risk for the higher return or capital gain he expects to realize by doing so.

Actually, all investment entails risk. Investment in Government
bonds involves the risk of depreciation of purchasing power of
the dollars in which interest and principal are payable, as well as
the risk of a rise in interest rates that would cause marketable
bonds to depreciate in price. Investment in equities involves the
risk that lower earnings and dividends or other developments
will depress the selling prices or reduce the income stocks will
provide. Only future events will determine which of these risks
is the greater.

Risk taking is unavoidable not only in investment, but in all
phases of economic life. The farmer who plants his crops, the
manufacturer and merchant who produce or buy goods for resale, all assume risks that they will not be able to sell their

products, that sales will have to be made at unprofitable prices, or
that other untoward developments will cause them loss.

The basic difference between investment and speculation is
thus mainly a matter of intent and knowledge of the person who
commits his funds. The investor wants to limit his risk so far as
is feasible. To do so effectively, he must either have the knowledge or obtain professional assistance to identify and avoid risks
in acquiring and holding securities. The speculator, on the other
hand, consciously assumes risks because he believes that pro-
spective profits are large enough to justify his doing so.

These considerations indicate that both investment and speculation can be conducted by either outright cash or margin purchases. The outright cash purchase of a security that involves a
large measure of known risk is a speculation; by the same token,
the purchase of securities involving little risk of loss would be
more in the nature of investment, even though made with the
help of a reasonable amount of borrowed money.

As a practical matter, most persons who invest their money
are not motivated exclusively by the desire either to avoid or
to incur risks. A large proportion of security purchases reflect
both investment and speculative motives. The use of borrowed
money to finance purchases is only one of many factors that
may characterize a particular purchase as an investment or a
speculation because of the motive of the buyer, and often it is
not a major distinguishing element.

Carrying Securities for Capital Gains

Securities may be bought with borrowed money for a quick
turnover or for longer periods. The New York Stock Exchange's
periodic Public Transaction Studies have provided some indication of the relative magnitude of each class of transaction, as
Chart III shows.

The June, 1959 study indicated that transactions designated
by the Exchange as "trading" in that they were, or probably
would be, closed out within 30 days amounted to 16.5% of all
share volume in margin accounts. Another 37.3% were "short-term

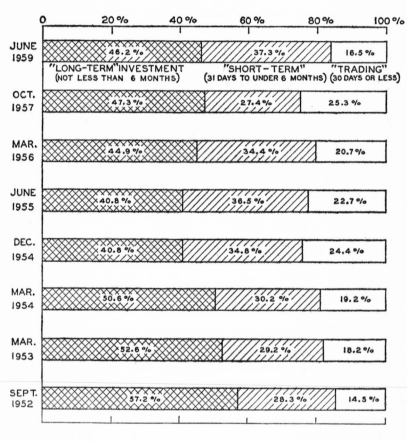

Chart III

INVESTMENT MOTIVATION OF PUBLIC
INDIVIDUAL MARGIN CUSTOMERS
1952–1959 *

* 1952, 1953, 1954—Estimated.

SOURCE: New York Stock Exchange *Public Transaction Studies.*

18

investment" transactions that were or probably would be closed out in from 30 days to less than 6 months; and 46.2% were "long-term investment" transactions that were or would be closed out in not less than 6 months.

These data, fragmentary as they are, point to the conclusion that much the larger part of the funds borrowed by investors and speculators at the time was being used to finance securities that they expected to carry or had carried for longer than a month, and almost half for holding securities that were to be carried for 6 months or longer.

Credit to Finance the Securities Business

A substantial proportion of outstanding security loans is utilized at all times to finance the conduct of the securities business, rather than for public investment and speculation.

Security dealers who originate, distribute and make markets in securities must carry costly inventories that are financed largely with bank borrowings. Such borrowing is greatly facilitated by the ability of security dealers to pledge the securities they carry in inventories as collateral for their loans.

By far the largest part of the credit required by the securities industry for its own business is needed to finance inventories of bond dealers making markets in U. S. Government, state, municipal and corporate obligations. The market for bonds is largely institutional in character. Dealers, to maintain ready markets, may be called upon at any time to buy or sell large blocks for their own account. Maintenance of substantial dealer inventories is necessary for the smooth functioning of such a market.

On July 1, 1959, reporting member banks of the Federal Reserve System had outstanding $293 million in loans to brokers and dealers secured by U. S. Government obligations. U. S. Government bond dealers also borrow from other banks, and obtain the equivalent of 100% loans on their inventory by selling securities to banks and corporations under repurchase agreements. Borrowings to carry inventories by dealers in state and municipal bonds can be estimated from the offerings contained in the daily

Blue List of Current Municipal Offerings, published in New York City. If it is assumed that the greater part of dealer inventories is being offered in this list and that 90% of the face value of these bonds is borrowed, some $230 million was being borrowed on June 30, 1959 to carry dealer inventories of outstanding tax-exempt bonds.

Data are not published on dealer inventories of corporate securities. On the basis of borrowings by member firms of the New York Stock Exchange, adjusted for borrowings on customer securities and identifiable borrowing for other purposes, security dealers other than stock exchange specialists and odd-lot dealers were borrowing $460 million to carry inventories of corporate securities on June 30, 1959.

Credit needs to finance security trading are minimized in the well-developed auction markets provided by the stock exchanges. Large dealer inventories are not needed to maintain close, active markets on the floor of a stock exchange. However, limited inventories are maintained by specialists and odd-lot dealers to facilitate the execution of orders. The New York Stock Exchange estimated that $80 million was being used by specialists and odd-lot dealers on all registered stock exchanges to carry firm positions in stocks in connection with these functions on June 30, 1959.

Financing New Issues

Credit is required also to clear payments in connection with the origination and distribution of new issues of securities.

The amounts borrowed at any time for underwriting and marketing new offerings vary widely with the volume of new financing and the speed with which new issues are distributed. In the first half of 1959, public offerings of corporate securities aggregated $5.0 billion and of state and municipal obligations $4.5 billion, according to the Securities and Exchange Commission. If we assume that underwriters and distributors carried such issues on the average of one week with 90% borrowings, approximately $330 million would have been borrowed on the average during the first half of 1959 to finance the vital function performed by the securities industry in the raising of new capital for industry and for state and local governments.

Credit may be needed by purchasers of new security issues, whether on privileged subscriptions or general public offerings, to complete payment for their purchases. Such borrowing gives the investor time to accumulate funds out of current income or by liquidation of other holdings to repay the loan.[1]

Wholesale vs. Retail Credit

Credit advanced to security dealers to conduct their business differs in several essential respects from borrowing to finance security purchases by the public.

Borrowings by security dealers to carry inventories are restricted by their ability to absorb the loss should the issues carried decline in price. This ability is determined by net worth. Hence, there is strong pressure on dealers to reduce inventories and repay borrowings by making price concessions whenever the volume of securities held expands substantially. By contrast, public speculative borrowing can swell to large proportions on occasion when conditions are popularly regarded as quite propitious for a major rise in stock prices.

There is a similarity between the financing of the securities business and financing of dealers in automobiles and other consumer durable goods. Loans to the dealers themselves to carry inventories for resale in each case can properly be described as "wholesale" financing. By the same token, credit advanced to customers to enable them to purchase either durable goods or securities constitutes "retail" credit.

In drawing a distinction between wholesale and retail uses of security credit, the reader should keep in mind that a large part of brokers' loans is used to finance customer purchases of securities, and so constitutes credit incurred at the wholesale level for retail purposes. The New York Stock Exchange has prepared comprehensive estimates of the use of credit and capital funds

---

[1] As a general rule, the Securities Exchange Act bars brokers and dealers from granting credit on a new issue in distribution, if they participated in the selling syndicate within the past 30 days.

TABLE I

ESTIMATED EMPLOYMENT OF CREDIT AND CAPITAL FUNDS
FOR THE PURPOSE OF PURCHASING AND/OR CARRYING SECURITIES
June 30, 1959

At Customers ("Retail") Level

Funds Available to Customers		Funds Employed by Customers	
Sources	*Estimated Amount (Millions)*	*Uses*	*Estimated Amount (Millions)*
Loans from:		General Margin Accounts:	
Brokers	$4,040	Brokers' Customers	$3,140
Banks	1,940	Banks' Customers	1,730
		Other Margin Accounts:	
		Subscription Accounts	80
		Purchase of U. S. Govt. securities	400
		Cash Purchases (by margin and cash customers)	630
Total[a]	$5,980		$5,980

At Brokers/Dealers' ("Wholesale") Level

Funds Available to Brokers/Dealers		Funds Employed by Brokers/Dealers	
Sources	*Estimated Amount (Millions)*	*Uses*	*Estimated Amount (Millions)*
Borrowings from:		Cash and Bank Balances	$ 680[b]
U. S. Banks	$2,320	To Finance Underwriting and Firm Positions:	
Foreign Agency Banks	850	Corporate (bonds and stock)	
Other Lenders	1,070	Specialists	60
Customers' Net Credit Balances	1,760	Odd-lot Dealers	20
Credit Balances in Firm and Partners' Accounts	160[c]	Other	540
"Housekeeping" functions	940[c, d]	Municipal Bonds	250
Capital (in investment, trading and profit & loss accounts of firms and partners)	1,340	U. S. Government Securities	1,820
		"Housekeeping" functions	1,030[c, e]
Less: Loans to Customers (non-wholesale activities)	−4,040		
Net financing of own transactions	$4,400		$4,400

---

a Excludes an indeterminate but believed to be negligible amount borrowed on life insurance policies, credit unions, savings bank passbooks, personal loans, etc.

b Includes commodity funds on deposit.

c These figures are for NYSE member firms only—there is no basis for estimating for purchasing and carrying securities at both the retail and wholesale levels. These estimates for June 30, 1959 are shown in Table I and Chart IV.

Business Purpose Loans on Security Collateral

A large volume of loans secured by stocks and bonds as collateral is made for business purposes. The amount of such loans cannot be determined from banking statistics, since only loans for "purchasing or carrying securities" are reported in the security loan figures. Some indications of the volume of other security loans, however, can be obtained from special surveys by Federal Reserve member banks.

The Federal Reserve banks made a survey of loans by 271 leading banks in early 1955 to determine how large a proportion of their loans of all kinds were secured by stocks and bonds. This was done at the request of Senator Fulbright, Chairman of the Senate Committee on Banking and Currency, for the Committee's study of the stock market. The survey indicated that loans on securities for purposes other than purchasing and carrying securities accounted for 5% of all loans by these banks, that "purpose" loans to brokers and dealers accounted for 7%, and "purpose" loans to other borrowers 3%. For all member banks of the Federal Reserve System, this survey concluded, "the total amount of such nonpurpose loans on securities collateral at all member banks was approximately $3 billion." [2]

The Board of Governors of the Federal Reserve System reported that, of total *business* loans by member banks aggregating

---

them for non-NYSE member firms.

d "Housekeeping" functions include: Securities borrowed, securities sold delivery pending, net debit balances of NYSE member & non-member firms; all other debit balances.

e "Housekeeping" functions include: Securities loaned, securities bought delivery pending, net credit balances of NYSE member & non-member firms; all other credit balances.

Source: Department of Research and Statistics, New York Stock Exchange.

[2] *Factors Affecting the Stock Market,* Staff Report to the Committee on Banking and Currency, U. S. Senate, 1955, p. 46.

Chart IV

ESTIMATED EMPLOYMENT OF CREDIT AND CAPITAL FUNDS FOR THE PURPOSE OF PURCHASING AND/OR CARRYING SECURITIES AS OF JUNE 30, 1959

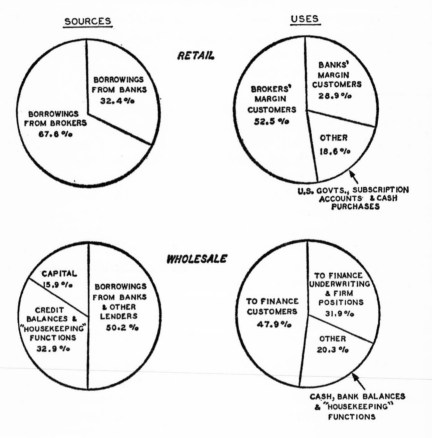

Figures may not add up to 100%, because of rounding.
SOURCE: New York Stock Exchange.

24

$30.8 billion on October 5, 1955, loans secured by U. S. Government securities amounted to $182 million, those secured by other bonds $165 million, and those secured by stocks slightly over $1 billion. Interest rates on business loans secured by stocks and bonds averaged materially lower, as is to be expected, than on such loans having other types of security.[3]

An unpublished survey of a small sample of banks in the New York Federal Reserve district in the summer of 1959 revealed that $63.8 million out of a total of $68.2 million of loans made to others than brokers and dealers "on readily marketable collateral" were classified as "non-purpose" loans. This suggests that the bulk of loans secured by listed stocks made by these commercial banks to others than brokers and dealers are classified as "non-purpose" loans.

An indeterminate amount of funds is doubtless borrowed from banks and other lenders, in some cases without stocks and bonds pledged as collateral, for the ultimate purpose of acquiring securities. Such borrowing will be considered in Chapter XI on Unregulated Sources of Security Credit.

No data are available on the extent to which security loans are used to finance consumption and personal expenditures caused by illness and similar emergencies. The availability of consumer credit in other forms tends to lessen the use of security collateral loans for such purposes, although interest rates are usually much lower where marketable securities are pledged as security for borrowing.

SUMMARY

The four main uses of loans secured by stock and bond collateral are (1) to finance investment and speculation in securities, (2) to finance the conduct of the securities business, (3) to facilitate and reduce the cost of business borrowing and (4) to facilitate and reduce the cost of consumer borrowing.

While the proportion of the total of such loans made for each purpose varies widely from time to time, each of the first three of these uses accounts for a substantial part.

---

[3] *Federal Reserve Bulletin*, September, 1959, pp. 1114-1129.

Loans made for "purchasing and carrying securities," as reported in banking statistics, include both credit advanced to finance investment and speculation and credit used to conduct the securities business. These two uses of security credit are as different in character as wholesale and retail credit used to finance the distribution of consumer durable goods that are sold eventually on the instalment plan.

Discussion of the economic role of security credit in Chapter IV will distinguish among loans made for these disparate purposes.

Chapter 3

SECURITY CREDIT FROM THE LENDER'S VIEWPOINT

From the viewpoint of lenders, loans are judged by their (1) safety, (2) liquidity and (3) interest return. Security loans rate very high in the first two respects, and in the third also when a strong demand for such credit lifts the rates paid by borrowers well above those prevailing on other types of loans.

Safety of Security Loans

Security loans are unique among the major types of bank lending in that they are secured by collateral, left in the lender's possession, with a ready, continuous market that can be checked at any time. Even loans secured by staple marketable commodities in transit or bonded warehouse do not enjoy comparable protection, because quality deterioration may affect the sales value of the commodities, and delays may occur in securing possession in the event of default on the loan.

The lender on securities, whether on call or time, has the right to call for additional margin promptly whenever the market value of the collateral declines below the specified ratio to the amount loaned. If the additional margin requested is not forthcoming within a reasonable time, the lender has the right to sell the collateral to reduce or pay off the loan, any excess realized over the amount due being paid to the borrower. Similarly, collateral can be sold to repay the loan, with interest due, if a time loan on securities is not paid off at its maturity, or when a deficiency in collateral is not made good, or a called demand loan is not repaid with reasonable promptness.

The high degree of safety these provisions give security loans, as well as the close financial supervision of its members by the New York Stock Exchange, explain the very favorable solvency record of Exchange member firms. This record has been considerably better than that of commercial banks or business enterprises since 1900. In the 21 years 1939-59, not a single member firm of the Exchange became insolvent. In view of the large sums that are constantly being loaned on securities to customers by member firms carrying margin accounts, this solvency record bears eloquent testimony to the quality of security loans, as well as to the effectiveness of supervision of the financial position of its members by the Exchange.

On June 30, 1959, Stock Exchange member firms carrying margin accounts reported that they had extended $3.5 billion of credit to their customers, whereas their own net worth was $610 million. The rest of the money required was borrowed from banks or was supplied by customers who had free credit balances. For the protection of their other customers as well as their creditors, therefore, Stock Exchange firms insist that margin accounts correct promptly a deficiency below minimum margin requirements. By doing so, they safeguard the quality of credit advanced by and to them for purchasing and carrying securities.

Many Stock Exchange firms apply minimum maintenance margin requirements even higher than the 25% requirement set by the New York Stock Exchange, to allow for rapid declines in stock prices and to provide for possible delays in complying with the Stock Exchange minimum requirement, in the event of a protracted stock market decline.

It goes without saying that the high quality of security credit is jeopardized whenever a lender fails to insist that a deficiency in collateral value be made good promptly. Commercial banks lending on collateral directly to customers have on occasion in the past taken an easy-going attitude in such cases to avoid antagonizing customers, and losses have resulted. As with other types of lending, the quality of a loan will deteriorate if protective provisions inserted to protect the lender against loss are not enforced when the need to do so arises.

Nevertheless, security loans as a class are recognized to have had a far better safety record than commercial, agricultural, real estate and consumer loans, the other major categories of bank lending. Supervisory officials state that losses on security loans to lending banks have been negligible in recent years, as banks have become more insistent on the maintenance of minimum margins set. Losses have been incurred almost exclusively in cases where decease of a borrower caused delay in the sale of collateral, because of the need to await legal authority to act for the account of the estate.

Liquidity of Security Loans

Liquidity is provided by assets that can be turned into cash promptly at any time without material loss to the owner.

Call loans on securities, based as they are on readily marketable collateral, have long been regarded as by far the most liquid type of bank loan. The reason for this is not only that pledged securities can be sold promptly if the borrower fails to pay off the loan when it is called. Even more important, over the long run, is the ready availability of other lenders to make a new loan if an outstanding loan should be called. Hence, a lender who calls a loan knows that the borrower can readily secure a new loan elsewhere to obtain funds to make payment, always provided that his collateral is adequate.

The shiftability of security loans among lenders, which greatly enhances their liquidity, is facilitated by the large number of commercial banks that make security loans. Loan brokers that bring borrowers and lenders together for a commission also may be utilized to find new lenders when outstanding security loans are called.

Before the establishment of the Federal Reserve System, as described in Chapter I, occasional brief "squeezes" occurred in the call money market due to concerted withdrawals of funds from New York by banks and others throughout the country. The "money panics" were caused by the great difficulty encountered by borrowers in arranging new loans to replace those that lending banks had to call to meet the demands made upon them by their depositors. The liquidity of call loans was not impaired, but interest rates were driven up to very high levels as borrowers sought to shift loans to other lenders while these episodes lasted. Since the establishment of the Federal Reserve System, which provides a ready source of liquidity for member banks all over the country, the need for concerted calling of security loans to meet withdrawals of funds from financial centers no longer exists. Hence, such call money squeezes no longer occur.

The elimination of the threat of periodic money panics and consequent wholesale forced liquidation on the stock exchanges has added to the attractiveness of security loans, and to that extent helps explain the expansion in such lending that followed the establishment of the Federal Reserve System.

Interest Rates on Security Loans

Ordinarily, banks make call loans on securities because of the high degree of safety and liquidity they provide. These qualities tend to attract an ample supply of funds to satisfy the demand for such credit, so that interest rates on call loans on securities have ruled considerably below other bank lending rates, as Chart V shows.

There have been times, however, when the supply of call money has fallen short of the demand. A heavy demand for business loans or an over-all credit stringency such as is caused by a restrictive Federal Reserve credit policy will limit the supply of call money. Should the demand for security loans be strong at such times, call money rates will rise well above those charged on other types of loans. This occurred during the "money panics" of the era before the establishment of the Federal Reserve System, and was last experienced in 1928 and 1929. At such times, loans on securities became attractive to lenders because of their higher rate of return, as well as their safety and liquidity. As a result, the supply of call money was expanded with large offerings from other lenders as well as banks.

These experiences demonstrated that the demand for security loans is "inelastic," as that term is used by economists, in that it is *relatively* insensitive to sharp increases in interest rates. When widespread confidence prevails that purchases of securi-

Chart V

SELECTED SHORT-TERM MONEY RATES
1947–1959

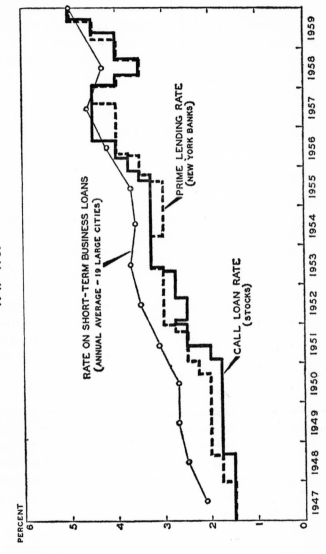

SOURCES: *Federal Reserve Bulletin; Bank and Quotation Record; Salomon Bros. & Hutzler.*

31

ties will prove profitable, demand for security credit becomes strong even at quite high interest rates.

Because margin regulation since 1934 has limited the effective demand for security loans in periods of vigorously advancing markets, interest rates on call loans have been relatively low as compared with other money market rates. Hence, banks have had only the incentives of quality and liquidity, but not of high yield, to make such loans. However, this has not been true for some other classes of lenders that are not subject to Federal Reserve margin regulations, as will be seen in Chapter XI on Unregulated Sources of Security Credit.

Place in Bank Portfolios

Security loans are attractive to commercial banks because of their safety and liquidity. The question has been raised from time to time whether these qualities, and the ease with which such loans can be made, do not cause banks to divert needed credit from business or agricultural borrowers to make security loans.

Commercial banks, as a matter of necessity, must seek at all times to satisfy the borrowing needs of their regular customers, particularly business concerns. Being dependent upon these customers for deposits and other types of business, the banks must favor them over other outlets in the allocation of loanable funds. In fact, a major reason why banks seek to maintain a high ratio of liquidity under ordinary conditions is to have loanable funds readily available to expand loans to their business customers when demand increases. At such times, banks tend to reduce call loans, holdings of U. S. Government securities and other "open market" types of assets to satisfy the borrowing needs of regular customers. This holds true particularly in periods when banks are short of reserves because a restrictive monetary policy is being pursued by the Federal Reserve System.

An added reason why business borrowers are favored is the fact that a part of the sum borrowed is left on deposit, increasing the effective rate of return to the bank. A number of banks expect average deposit balances of 20% of the amount borrowed by business customers. Such requirements are enforced more strictly at times of credit stringency.

Consumer loans give the advantage of a substantially higher average rate of interest than other classes of loans, including security loans.

Security loans by banks are often withdrawn in full when the loan is made, so that there is no offsetting deposit balance. It is true that brokerage firms that borrow regularly from a bank are expected to maintain compensating balances. In a period of tight money like 1959, a number of commercial banks in financial centers required borrowing brokerage houses to maintain deposit balances of 10 or 15% of the amount of call loans. However, offsetting deposits required in connection with security loans tend to be materially lower than those asked of business borrowers.

Among bank liquidity media, U. S. Government securities possess two advantages over call loans on securities. Regarded as minimum risk assets by the supervisory authorities, they are excluded in computing the ratio of capital funds to so-called "risk assets." Call loans, on the other hand, are conventionally included with "risk assets" in computing the ratio of capital funds to assets at risk. U. S. Government securities also can be pledged at any time by member banks as security for advances from the Federal Reserve banks.

SUMMARY

Security loans, having the protection of readily marketable collateral in the lender's possession, enjoy a very high degree of safety. Call loans on securities are also highly liquid, because substitute lenders are readily available to the borrower if his loan should be called. Should a borrower fail to repay a called loan, pledged securities can be sold promptly to provide the funds for doing so.

Interest rates on call loans on securities ordinarily rule below those on other types of bank loans. However, when an active demand for such loans develops, rates may rise to a high level as borrowers bid for additional loanable funds.

Commercial banks find security loans quite attractive because of their safety and liquidity characteristics. Nevertheless, banks tend to favor commercial borrowers in times of credit stringency, because of the deposits and other profitable business they provide. Consumer loans are favored because of their high rates of return. As a liquidity medium, short-term Government securities possess some advantage over call loans on securities.

Chapter 4

EFFECTS OF SECURITY CREDIT ON THE ECONOMY

Security credit affects both the growth and the stability of the economy.

By facilitating the process of capital formation, security loans foster economic growth and stability. On the few occasions when quite large increases or decreases occur in the volume of outstanding security credit within a relatively short period of time, however, the stability of the economy is affected adversely.

Facilitating Capital Formation

The most important economic role of security credit is to facilitate capital formation.

The chief difference between a developed and an underdeveloped economy is the extent and character of the productive facilities or capital goods that are available to provide the goods and services required by the population. The process of capital formation is essential to the growth and health of every economy that has advanced beyond the primitive stage.

Capital formation consists of two steps—saving and the investment of savings in capital goods. Through saving, a part of current income is withheld from consumption and made available for investment. When savings are invested in capital goods—directly in business enterprises, through financial institutions or through the purchase of securities—the process of capital formation is completed.

Security credit facilitates the process of capital formation in the following ways:

1. *Providing funds to finance the underwriting and distribu-*

tion of securities. Security flotations enable corporations and governments to attract savings from individuals and financial institutions and to utilize them to acquire productive facilities. The financing of new security issues is made possible by security loans to underwriters and distributors, whose own funds are relatively small by comparison with the volume of securities they distribute.

2. *Furnishing funds to finance the business of security brokers and dealers who provide markets for outstanding issues.* Without a market on which securities can be sold readily whenever that becomes desirable or necessary, the public's savings could not be expected to flow in large volume into the long-term bonds or stocks that are issued to finance capital formation. Brokers and dealers in securities provide such a market.

3. *Providing funds to purchasers of securities who are willing to assume the risk of buying stocks and bonds with borrowed funds.* When used to finance purchases of new issues of securities, security loans supplement or anticipate the investment of savings. When used to finance purchases of outstanding securities, security loans enable the sellers of such issues in turn to use the money to buy newly offered stocks or bonds, to make direct investments in business enterprises, or to buy goods for consumption.

Marketing of securities of less seasoned and of smaller enterprises, which do not appeal to institutional investors, in particular may be facilitated because purchasers can utilize security credit, directly or indirectly, to help pay for such issues.

4. *Broadening the market for corporate stockholders so that they can sell part or all of their holdings at prices that will reflect growth in value due to the productive use of retained profits.* The larger part of corporate capital formation is financed with retained earnings rather than by the sale of new security issues. Department of Commerce data on the uses and sources of corporate funds show that in the decade 1950-59 internal sources provided 62% of the $375 billion required for corporate financial needs. Corporate stockholders are willing to have so large a proportion of the cash flow reinvested in the business rather than paid out to them, because market prices over the

long run tend to reflect the added value that retained earnings impart to their shares. This results from the fact that the investment of retained profits in productive facilities increases earnings per share and so makes possible the payment of higher dividends eventually.

Security credit broadens the market for corporate shares by enabling many persons to buy and hold stocks with the aid of borrowed money. A broader market tends to make prices reflect more accurately all elements of value, including the benefits stockholders derive from the retention and reinvestment of profits on their behalf. Security credit, in other words, facilitates capital formation through corporate savings, as well as through individual savings.

Without the ready availability of security loans, the volume of capital formation would be curtailed and, as a result, economic growth would be hampered. Moreover, in an advanced economy geared to a relatively high level of capital formation, maintenance of a high rate of investment becomes essential to economic stability as well as to growth. Curtailment of capital expenditures has been a primary cause of business recessions.

Providing Liquidity

Liquidity is essential to the healthy functioning of a developed economy.

Liquidity provides funds to take prompt advantage of new opportunities and to make new investments that contribute to economic growth. Liquidity also lessens pressure to liquidate assets, often at considerable sacrifice, and to curtail expenditures when economic prospects become clouded, developments which contribute greatly to economic instability. The ability to borrow on securities enables the owners to raise funds without having to sell securities at prices that are considered unattractive and that may entail substantial losses.

Security loans provide one important source of liquidity to the economy. Member banks of the Federal Reserve System borrow from the Federal Reserve banks chiefly through advances secured by U. S. Government obligations. Businesses and individuals can raise funds by borrowing on securities, in amounts and on terms that would not be available to them without such collateral.

The fact that funds can be obtained by pledging securities as collateral for loans at any time is even more important as a source of liquidity than the amount of security loans that is actually outstanding. The amount of cash and the equivalent that financial institutions, businesses and individuals feel they must hold to assure needed liquidity is substantially reduced because of their ability to borrow on securities owned whenever the need should arise.

Availability of collateral loans, by broadening the market for securities, contributes to liquidity also by enhancing the marketability of securities owned, so that cash can be raised so much more readily by their sale.

Effects of Security Loan Expansion

The economic effects of an expansion of security loans become clear when one considers how security markets function.

Security markets provide a mechanism for bringing buyers and sellers of securities together. Therefore, they do not absorb funds, as has too often been erroneously assumed. Rather, they act as a conduit by which funds are transferred from the buyers to the sellers of securities.[1] The relative stability and small amount of the cash balances held by New York Stock Exchange member firms is empirical proof of the market's role as a conduit for funds, rather than as a reservoir absorbing funds from other sectors of the economy, as was formerly assumed by many to be the case. Chart VI shows that cash balances of member firms carrying margin accounts varied within a relatively narrow range—around $300 to $400 million—during the past decade. The volume of customer credit to purchase and carry securities, on the other hand, varied from less than $2 billion to more than $5 billion during this period.

---

[1] For discussion of this point, see Fritz Machlup, *The Stock Market, Credit and Capital Formation* (London: Wm. Hodge & Co., Ltd., 1940); and Charles A. Dice and Wilford J. Eiteman, *The Stock Market* (New York: McGraw-Hill Book Company, 1941), pp. 373-5.

Chart VI

CASH BALANCES,*
MEMBER FIRMS OF THE NEW YORK STOCK EXCHANGE
CARRYING MARGIN ACCOUNTS
1951–1959 †

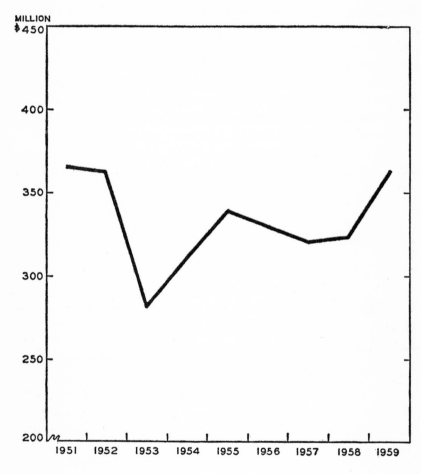

* Cash on hand and in banks.
† June 30.
SOURCE: New York Stock Exchange.

When an expansion of security loans occurs, the additional funds borrowed by purchasers of securities are promptly turned over to the sellers. The economic consequences of an increase in loans, therefore, is determined by what these sellers of securities do with the money they receive.

Where the sellers of securities who receive the funds borrowed by the security purchasers are corporations that have floated new issues, the increase in security loans finances capital formation by these corporations. Should the sellers be individuals who utilize part or all of the proceeds of the sale to make a down payment on new homes or to buy automobiles, security loan expansion finances the acquisition of consumer durable goods.

In either event, the expansion of security loans increases spending for business or consumption purposes just as would loans incurred specifically for business or consumption.

The notion that security loans divert funds from business *in the aggregate* is a fallacy. It ignores the obvious fact that, for each dollar of net increase in outstanding security loans, roughly a dollar is withdrawn by sellers of securities for business or consumption purposes. This fact helps to explain why periods of rapid expansion of security loans are characterized by marked business prosperity.

It is true, however, that an expansion of security loans might make it more difficult *for particular concerns* to borrow if commercial banks that increase their security lending were to curtail their business lending in consequence. Instances of this could happen in a period of credit stringency. But commercial banks generally favor their regular business borrowers under such conditions, because of added benefits they derive from such customers. In any event, margin regulation now limits the demand for security loans, and so prevents a shift of loanable funds by commercial banks from business to security loans even in this limited sense.

Qualitative Effects on the Economy

The quantitative effect on the economy of an expansion of security loans tends to be the same as an expansion of other forms of credit. The funds borrowed, going to sellers of securities who withdraw the proceeds of sale from the security markets, will be used ultimately for business or consumption spending, and so stimulate economic activity.

But there may be differences in the qualitative effects of security and other types of credit expansion. A major advance in stock prices may cause a number of security owners to take profits and raise their standard of living. When the securities purchased from them are paid for with borrowed money in large part, security loan expansion goes to finance luxury consumption. Money borrowed to buy a security might ultimately go to purchase a high-priced car, for example, whereas a business loan of equal amount might be used to buy a machine tool. This could distort the pattern of spending in the economy for a time, with an adverse effect on economic stability.

Moreover, lenders exert far less influence on the uses to which security credit is put than on most other types of credit extension. In the case of business or consumer borrowing, the lender is ordinarily told the economic use to which the funds will be put, and his decision to lend may be affected by this knowledge. In the case of loans incurred to buy securities, on the other hand, the funds will be spent by the sellers of the securities. Except in the case of new issues, the lender will know neither the identity nor the objectives of such sellers. Only where security owners borrow on securities they already own for specified business or personal purposes is the lender aware of the economic uses to which the funds borrowed are to be put.

Differences in the qualitative effects upon the economy of expansion of security and of other types of credit become less significant, however, when the secondary effects of credit expansion are taken into consideration. A rapid expansion of any type of credit—not security loans only—tends to stimulate the whole economy, causing expansion of spending in a number of directions that may be non-sustainable.

Effects of Security Loan Contraction

The economic effects of a contraction of security loans are the reverse of the effects of an expansion.

Security loans are reduced either because the debtors use funds on hand to repay such borrowings or because securities carried with credit are sold to cash buyers. Such sales may occur voluntarily, or they may result from the inability of holders to meet margin calls in a declining market. In either event, funds used to pay off security loans become unavailable for other uses, so that business and consumption spending tend to be reduced.

A contraction of security loans, as of other borrowings, reduces the volume of funds available for current expenditure. Each dollar of net repayment of any type of loan tends to reduce by roughly one dollar spending for business or consumption purposes. This is one reason why periods of rapid contraction of security loans have often been periods of business recession.

Pyramiding and Anti-Pyramiding Effects

One aspect of the behavior of security credit that may affect the stability of the economy is the so-called pyramiding effect. This is the ability of security owners to borrow increased amounts as a result of a rise in prices of the issues they own.

When security prices rise, in part because of purchases effected with the help of borrowed money, the owners are placed in position to buy more securities on margin. Such purchases, in turn, tend to raise prices further and so increase again the ability of security owners to borrow.

Essentially the same thing occurs when other forms of borrowing raise prices of commodities or other property, or when business borrowing raises the level of business activity and profits, and so increases the credit worthiness of borrowers. However, at times such as the late 1920's the pyramiding effect that accompanies the increased use of security credit is particularly marked. And since expansion of security credit—as of other forms of credit—causes a corresponding expansion of business and consumption spending, business activity may be powerfully stimulated in consequence.

Such stimulation can contribute largely to business instability because of its temporary character. Whenever the expansion of security credit halts, the stimulus is withdrawn, a development that could make the subsequent contraction of business activity so much more pronounced.

Far more significant, however, may be the anti-pyramiding effect of a contraction of security credit that tends to follow a period of major expansion. Sales of securities to meet margin calls reduce the ability of owners to borrow, and lead to new margin calls. Putting up money to meet margin calls, or to buy securities from owners who sell because they are unable or unwilling to put up more margin, diverts purchasing power from business or consumption uses. Security loan contraction thus tends to contract business activity.

A decline in market prices rather than the credit worthiness of the borrower governs the issuance of margin calls. Consequently, at a time when a large volume of security loans is outstanding on relatively thin margins, the anti-pyramiding effect can be a good deal more pronounced than that which arises from a contraction of other forms of credit.

SUMMARY

Under ordinary conditions, when the magnitude of changes in the volume of security loans outstanding is relatively small, the chief economic effects of security credit are to facilitate capital formation and to enhance liquidity.

It is only when major increases or decreases in the volume of such loans occur that they affect the stability of the economy to a material extent. A large-scale expansion or contraction of security credit tends to stimulate or depress business activity as much as would the expansion or contraction of other types of credit. The effect may be greater because pronounced increases in security prices can lead to a pyramiding of security credit, while a decline in security prices has an anti-pyramiding effect on such borrowing.

Because large increases or decreases in security credit affect the economy like corresponding changes in the volume of commercial, agricultural or consumer credit, security loan expansion and contraction have a significant bearing on credit control. This is discussed in the next chapter.

Chapter 5

SECURITY LOANS AND CREDIT CONTROL

The Role of Credit Control

The bulk of the money supply of an economically advanced country consists of demand deposits in banks. Such deposits are created in the main by loans and investments of commercial banks. Hence, the money supply can be regulated through control over lending and investing by commercial banks.

Control over the availability and cost of bank credit has come to be regarded, in fact, as essential for the health of a free enterprise economy. By relying heavily upon credit control to moderate booms and recessions and to help maintain a sustainable rate of growth, more direct Government intervention and management of the economy can be avoided.

Chairman William McChesney Martin of the Board of Governors of the Federal Reserve System has described the primary objectives of credit control as follows:

> The Federal Reserve's responsibility is primarily for relating the availability of bank credit to the needs of sustainable growth of the economy. The aim of the Federal Reserve is to see that banks have, or can readily obtain, reserves that are adequate for these needs but not in excess of them.[1]

Again, he said:

> The Federal Reserve System will continue to the best of its ability to contribute, so far as it can, to continuing prosperity and economic growth, without inflation.[2]

Economic growth is fostered by making loans readily available to credit-worthy borrowers at reasonable interest rates. This the

---

[1] Statement before the House Select Committee on Small Business, Nov. 21, 1957.
[2] Statement before the Joint Economic Committee, Feb. 6, 1959.

Federal Reserve System does by providing reserves to member banks sufficient to support an upward long-run trend in bank loans and investment.

At certain times, however, excessive optimism stimulated by favorable economic conditions may generate a demand for loans so large as to produce an inflationary boom. If funds continue to be freely available to all credit-worthy borrowers at such times, economic growth would be accelerated, but the pace could not be sustained. Excess productive capacity and inventories would be built up, and this in time would lead to a period of recession marked by lessened spending, inventory liquidation and increased unemployment. Economic instability results when the economy grows at a rate or in a manner that is not sustainable.

To promote economic stability, central banks pursue a policy of "leaning against the wind." This calls for restriction of bank credit in times of prosperity and boom, and stimulation of expansion of loans and investments when recessions develop.

This chapter considers the ways in which borrowing on securities may influence the effectiveness of credit control.

Quantitative or Qualitative Controls

A central bank like the Federal Reserve System can seek to control either the total volume of bank loans and investments or particular kinds of credit extension. The first approach is known as general or quantitative credit control; the second constitutes selective or qualitative control.

Experience has shown that control over credit can be effective over the whole economy only if it is conducted on a quantitative basis. If only certain types of lending are regulated, while the total volume of bank loans and investments is permitted to expand and contract without control, the stability of the economy may be undermined and economic growth checked or reversed for a time.

A number of experiences have demonstrated the primary importance of quantitative or over-all credit control. A classic example occurred in the spring of 1929. The Federal Reserve System was then pursuing a restrictive credit policy to restrain the boom. The discount rate of the Federal Reserve Bank of New York was raised to 6% to discourage bank lending. At the same time, however, the Bank reduced its acceptance buying rate to 5% in the belief that this step would maintain an adequate supply of funds to finance foreign trade, even though other types of credit were being restricted.

But the legal reserves that some member banks obtained by selling acceptances to the Federal Reserve Bank at the lower rate enabled them to expand their loans and investments. As funds were paid out by these banks, reserves of other banks increased, permitting a multiple expansion of loans and investments by the member banks as a whole on the basis of reserves obtained by selling acceptances to the Federal Reserve Bank. Thus, the lower acceptance buying rate defeated the purpose of a higher rediscount rate, so that credit control was made ineffective by failure to concentrate on its quantitative aspect.[3]

The Federal Reserve banks cannot encourage expansion of some types of loans, discourage other kinds of lending, and at the same time exert effective control over the total volume of bank credit. Since bank deposits expand and contract with total loans and investments, regardless of the types of loans and investments made by the banks, the Federal Reserve authorities must necessarily be concerned primarily with quantitative credit control.

Quantitative Credit Control and Security Loans

Quantitative or over-all credit control, the chief means of regulating the money supply in a free enterprise economy, affects the several types of credit extension differently. Such quantitative credit control is exercised through Federal Reserve open market

---

[3] "There is no identifying mark on member-bank reserves obtained at the acceptance window as compared to those obtained through discounts," E. A. Goldenweiser wrote in his book on *American Monetary Policy* (New York: McGraw-Hill Book Company, 1951). "The funds can be used for any purpose desired by the member banks, including the then frowned-upon loans to brokers, and the banking system as a whole can extend credit aggregating several times the amount of the additional reserves."

operations in Government securities, changes in legal reserve requirements of the member banks and discount rate changes.

Under *ordinary* conditions, security loans are responsive to quantitative credit controls. Commercial banks prefer to serve the needs of their regular business customers in a period of credit stringency, and so will seek at such times to limit loans they make to purchase or carry securities. Some investors and speculators who borrow to purchase or carry securities are likely to be discouraged by higher interest rates and lessened availability of loans, particularly those who count on the differential between the income received on pledged securities and the interest paid on loans. In fact, at times when the security markets are dull or declining, high interest rates on such borrowing may lead to the liquidation of many loans to purchase or carry securities. For example, between June and October, 1957, a period of high interest rates and declining stock prices, customer borrowings from stock exchange houses and banks to carry securities other than U. S. Government bonds declined from $4.0 billion to $3.6 billion, a drop of 10%. Similarly, during the first four months of 1960, when the call loan rate was 5½% and stock prices were declining, customer borowings fell 7% from $4.5 billion to $4.2 billion.

Normally, quantitative credit control thus is effective in regulating the volume of security loans, as well as of other types of credit.

There are occasions, however, when over-all credit controls have little effect upon the trend of security loans. This is true when favorable economic conditions foster widespread confidence that security prices are going to advance substantially. Many security buyers are then quite ready to borrow at high interest rates in order to carry larger amounts of securities for the rise. The interest paid on security loans, whatever the rate, seems at such times to be relatively small by comparison with the capital gains expected. When borrowers offer to pay high enough rates of interest on security loans, large amounts of additional loanable funds are attracted. If commercial banks do not expand security lending at such times, other lenders will do so.

Effect on Quantitative Control

On occasions when widespread optimism about the outlook for security prices gives rise to a very strong demand for security loans, a rapid expansion of security credit could undermine the effectiveness of quantitative credit control. This happened during the late 1920's.

Under such conditions, quite high interest rates offered by borrowers will attract loanable funds from a variety of sources. In October, 1929, to take the most extreme occurrence of this kind, loans to brokers and dealers by nonbank lenders were more than twice as large as loans from banks, the usual source of these loans. As a result, the total volume of loans being extended expanded at a rapid rate—at the very time that the Federal Reserve authorities were trying to restrict lending.

Following the period of rapid expansion of security loans in the late 1920's, such credit contracted severely in the 1930-32 period when the Federal Reserve authorities were seeking to check the contraction of credit generally as their policy objective.

During the history of the Federal Reserve System, only in the period from 1926 to 1932 could the expansion and contraction of security credit be considered to have interfered with the effectiveness of quantitative credit control. This has been a rare development in terms of historical experience. Since 1934, selective control through margin regulation has barred the possibility of a repetition of that isolated episode.

The Pyramiding Effect

Another factor that lessens the effectiveness of over-all or quantitative credit controls in regulating the volume of security loans is the tendency of borrowers to pyramid their borrowings on a rising security market, the economic effects of which were discussed in the preceding chapter. Describing this tendency as it was manifested in 1929, E. A. Goldenweiser wrote that "as stock prices advance, these stocks become acceptable collateral for larger loans." [4]

---

[4] Goldenweiser, *op. cit.*, pp. 150-1.

This pyramiding effect develops in all types of credit granting, but it tends to be much more pronounced in security credit. The broad, active market for stocks and bonds makes both borrowers and lenders promptly aware that a basis exists for increased credit extension when prices of the pledged securities rise. Table II shows how higher initial margin requirements check this pyramiding effect.

Quantitative credit control is equally ineffective in maintaining or expanding the volume of security loans when adverse economic prospects cause the stock market to decline and foster pessimism about the outlook for stock prices. Then security loans tend to be liquidated, even if a credit policy of active ease and low interest rates is being pursued by the Federal Reserve authorities. Under such conditions, borrowers become much more concerned with avoiding losses on the securities they hold than with the cost or availability of security loans. Moreover, as price declines impair margins, forced selling brings about a contraction of security credit.

Because falling prices reduce the amounts owners can borrow on their securities, the pyramiding effect is experienced in reverse when the stock market declines persistently. Table III shows how higher initial margin requirements act to prevent this anti-pyramiding effect.

Periods of pronounced stock market strength or weakness thus tend to be exceptions to the normal tendency of security loans to be responsive to general or quantitative credit controls. This arises in large part from the tendency of the stock market to act as a barometer that reflects future prospects for the economy as appraised by investors and traders, rather than current circumstances such as the rate of interest charged on security loans.

Qualitative Credit Control

While experience has shown that quantitative credit control must be the primary instrument for carrying out Federal Reserve policy, some qualitative or selective controls also have been applied.

The original Federal Reserve Act contained qualitative ele-

TABLE II

How Higher Margins Reduce Pyramiding in a Rising Market
(Based on original equity of $1,000)

(1) Margin	(2) Value of Securities Purchased	(3) If prices rise from $100 a share to:	(4) Equity after Price Change	(5) Value of Securities that could be held with new Equity (Col. 4 ÷ Col. 1)	(6) Possible Borrowing after Price Change (Col. 5 — Col. 4)
10%	$10,000	$110	$2,000	$20,000	$18,000
		150	6,000	60,000	54,000
50%	2,000	110	1,200	2,400	1,200
		150	2,000	4,000	2,000
70%	1,400 (rounded)	110	1,140	1,630	490
		150	1,700	2,430	730
90%	1,100 (rounded)	110	1,110	1,230	120
		150	1,550	1,720	170

TABLE III

How Higher Margins Lessen Liquidation in a Falling Market
(Based on original equity of $1,000)

(1) Margin	(2) Value of Securities Purchased	(3) If prices drop from $100 a share to:	(4) Equity after Price Change	(5) Value of Securities that could be held with new Equity (Col. 4 ÷ Col. 1)	(6) Possible Borrowing after Price Change (Col. 5 — Col. 4)
10%	$10,000	$90	0	0	0
		50	0	0	0
50%	2,000	90	$800	$1,600	$800
		50	0	0	0
70%	1,400 (rounded)	90	860	1,230	370
		50	300	430	130
90%	1,100 (rounded)	90	890	990	100
		50	450	500	50

ments. Thus, security loans by member banks were made ineligible for rediscount privileges at the Federal Reserve banks, while specially favorable treatment was accorded agricultural loans and bankers' acceptances. However, these provisions reflected a bias for or against particular types of bank lending, rather than an effort to make over-all credit control more effective by supplementary qualitative measures.

The Federal Reserve authorities have also sought to exert qualitative control over credit on occasion through pronouncements directed to member banks or the public at large. An example of such "moral suasion" was the statement on "Guides to Credit Policy" contained in the annual report of the Federal Reserve Board for 1923, in which it was stated that Federal Reserve credit should be limited to agricultural, industrial and commercial purposes. Another example was the request to member banks to limit their loans to security brokers in 1928 and 1929, a move that was designed to make quantitative control more effective at the time.

The issue of qualitative control over a particular type of credit arose again as a result of wide swings in prices of Government securities in 1957-58, which were intensified by heavy purchases on thin margins and through repurchase agreements. A Treasury-Federal Reserve study of that episode found that

> . . . at times an undue amount of speculation financed on thinly margined credit can be detrimental to the market and competition of lenders in extending credit to prospective holders may result in deterioration in appropriate equity margin standards. This experience raises the question of the need for some action to assure that sound credit standards will be consistently maintained by lenders in credit extension backed by Government securities and also to keep the total volume of such credit from expanding unduly at times.
>
> The chief objective of qualitative control over lending on Government securities, as contemplated in this study, would be the prevention of "wide and rapid price fluctuations in the Government securities market" because of their impact on "Treasury debt management responsibilities".[5]

Legal authority to exert direct selective control over a partic-

---

[5] See summary of the Treasury-Federal Reserve Study in the *Federal Reserve Bulletin*, August, 1959, pp. 860-876.

ular kind of credit extension was first given the Federal Reserve authorities by the Securities Exchange Act of 1934, which provided for the regulation of major types of lending to purchase and carry securities. During World War II and up to 1947, between September, 1948 and June, 1949, and again in the Korean War period, regulation of consumer loans and, between 1950 and 1952, of real estate mortgage lending was authorized. With the ending of consumer and real estate credit controls in 1952, qualitative control by the Federal Reserve System was limited to the regulation of loans for purchasing and carrying securities.

Arguments for Qualitative Control of Security Loans

The arguments advanced for selective, qualitative control for security loans are:

1. Over-all credit controls cannot be counted upon to check a rapid expansion of security loans when speculative enthusiasm is rampant and borrowers are willing to pay very high rates of interest for such credit.

2. High interest rates offered by borrowers, in turn, can attract sufficient funds to satisfy an expanding demand for security credit because of the safety and liquidity of such loans. If banks will not increase such lending, other lenders will do so at high interest rates.

3. Since funds borrowed on securities, when spent by security sellers, swell business or consumer spending, an expansion of security loans may stimulate economic activity at the very time that the Federal Reserve authorities are pursuing a policy of restraint to check a boom. In periods like 1928 and 1929, the rapid expansion of security loans tended to neutralize the restrictive credit policy then being applied, and so to make quantitative credit control ineffective for too long a time.

4. The rapid and, at times, forced liquidation of security loans that follows the culmination of a stock market boom similarly tends to neutralize an easy money policy, and could have some restraining effect upon economic activity when the Federal

Reserve authorities seek to spur recovery through over-all credit expansion.[6]

5. Raising margin requirements when stock prices rise and lowering such requirements when prices fall contribute to stability of stock prices, and thereby to over-all economic stability.

The first four of these arguments relate selective control over security loans to making quantitative credit control more effective, and so conform to the prevailing view that effective quantitative control of credit is by far the most important instrument of monetary policy.

The argument that security credit should be regulated to promote greater stock market stability is far more dubious, especially since it assumes that those who administer the regulation must decide that stock prices are too high or too low at particular levels, or that a given advance or decline in stock prices is too rapid. This argument actually goes beyond the sphere of credit control and into the far more questionable area of influencing the behavior of stock prices.

Arguments Against Qualitative Credit Control

A number of arguments have been advanced from time to time against selective control of security credit. These include:

1. Selective controls are less consistent with a free enterprise system than general controls. The extent to which each type of credit is used should be determined by the forces of supply and demand in the market place, with Federal Reserve actions limited to general or quantitative control.

2. All types of credit are subject to occasional exaggerated

---

[6] This argument was stated by Dr. E. A. Goldenweiser as follows:

"One more observation about 1929. It was a remarkable demonstration of the fact that loans which are entirely safe for the lenders may not be safe for borrowers and may be dangerous for the community. The collapse of the stock market in 1929 was followed by an abrupt decline in security loans. . . . These stock market losses and the resultant depletion of funds which would have been used for consumption or business purposes were factors that aggravated the course of the depression which began to develop at the end of 1929." Goldenweiser, *op. cit.*, p. 155.

expansion or contraction which contributes to economic instability. Hence, a case could be made, based on particular past experiences, for qualitative control over every type of loan—leading to detailed Government management of all credit extension.

3. Since selective controls of consumer and real estate mortgage lending have been terminated, retention of selective control for security loans alone discriminates unfairly against this particular type of credit.

4. Selective control of security loans is limited to certain types of credit extension by some lenders on some kinds of securities. Hence, it affects some borrowers and lenders in this field and not others, with consequent lessened effectiveness of control and inequities as between borrowers.

Consumer and Security Credit Compared

Consumer and security credit have some features in common. Consumer loans at all times, and security loans on occasion, yield high rates of interest to lenders that cause them to be less sensitive to quantitative credit control measures. Both types of credit are regarded critically by those who hold to the classical doctrine that banks should limit their lending, so far as practicable, to productive, self-liquidating purposes. Hence, termination of selective control of consumer credit by Congress in 1952 has set a precedent, it has been suggested, for similar action with regard to security credit control.

There are basic differences, however, between the two types of credit.

Lenders making consumer loans, to protect themselves from loss, must check carefully on the ability of individual borrowers to repay when due. Where adequate collateral is pledged for security loans, by contrast, the ability of the borrowers to repay the loans is not a limiting consideration in extending credit.

Similarly, consumers become reluctant to increase their borrowings when repayments due approach an amount that they cannot readily meet from income or other resources. But those who borrow to purchase and carry securities may expand their loans without relation to their personal ability to repay when rising collateral values enable them to borrow more and the prospect of further price advances makes such borrowing seem attractive.

There are thus factors restraining both lenders and borrowers from expanding consumer credit unduly that do not apply at times to the expansion of security credit.[7]

SUMMARY

Credit control by the Federal Reserve System plays a vital role in fostering sustainable economic growth without inflation.

Only when monetary management has been conducted on an over-all or quantitative basis has it been effective.

Security lending has ordinarily been responsive to quantitative credit control. However, on occasions when economic conditions have created widespread expectations of a sharp rise in security prices, security loans have expanded rapidly in the face of a restrictive over-all credit policy. At such times, borrowers have been willing to pay high rates of interest for security loans, and the high quality of such loans attracts loanable funds in large volume. The pyramiding effect of a rise of security prices on ability to borrow contributes to the unresponsiveness of security loans to over-all credit restriction.

The chief argument for qualitative control of security credit is that it is needed to make quantitative credit control more effective on an occasion such as 1928-29, rare as such episodes have been in our economic history. On that occasion, the rapid expansion of security loans—in the face of a restrictive over-all credit policy—tended to undermine the effectiveness of quantitative credit control.

The need for qualitative control of security credit is thus related to the magnitude of such loans. The latter subject is discussed in the following chapter.

---

[7] See Board of Governors of the Federal Reserve System, *Consumer Instalment Credit* (Washington: Government Printing Office, 1957), especially Part III.

Chapter 6

MAGNITUDE OF SECURITY CREDIT

While credit is essential for the normal functioning and healthy growth of an economy, an excessive expansion of credit in the aggregate or of particular classes of credit can undermine economic stability.

Qualitative control of security lending by the Board of Governors of the Federal Reserve System was inaugurated to prevent excessive expansion of one type of credit—security loans. To accomplish this purpose, accurate data on the magnitude of security loans and yardsticks for judging whether such lending is becoming excessive are essential. A given volume of security loans may be considered to be large at one time, but relatively small at a later date because economic growth has caused a major expansion of credit outstanding and of aggregate security values.

Yardsticks for judging the relative magnitude of security loans are:

1. Historical comparisons.
2. Comparisons with other classes of private debt.
3. The ratio of security loans of banks to total bank loans.
4. The ratio of security credit outstanding to the aggregate value of outstanding stocks.
5. The relation between changes in security loans and changes in the aggregate market value of securities.

To apply these yardsticks, reliable statistics to measure the volume of security loans are required. Unfortunately, no inclusive single statistical measure of security credit is available, due to overlapping of coverage by each group of statistics.

Measuring Security Credit

Three main groups of statistics are available for measuring the volume of security loans. These are:

1. *Security loans by banks,* both to brokers and dealers and to other borrowers. Statistics of demand loans secured by stock and bond collateral have been published for national banks for each year since 1881 by the Comptroller of the Currency. Data on security loans of member banks of the Federal Reserve System, of insured banks and of all commercial banks have been published for more recent periods by bank supervisory agencies. The New York Stock Exchange has prepared inclusive estimates of security loans by all banks in the United States, including private banks, going back to 1939, shown in Table IV.[1]

Since the end of 1958, foreign bank agencies in New York have been reporting the amount of their security loans to the New York State Banking Department. These statistics have not been published to date. An indication of their magnitude is given by the amounts borrowed by New York Stock Exchange member firms carrying margin accounts from U. S. agencies of foreign banks, reported at $605 million for June 30, 1959 in the September, 1959, issue of the *Federal Reserve Bulletin.* Other security brokers and dealers, it was estimated at the time, accounted for another $200 to $250 million of borrowings from foreign bank agencies, on the basis of statistics on security loans made by Canadian banks in non-Canadian funds.

2. *Borrowings by members of the New York Stock Exchange,* from both banks and other lenders. By including borrowings by Exchange members from sources other than banks, this series covers other ground than the statistics of security loans by banks shown in Table IV.

---

[1] This estimate is based on statistics of loans by banks in the United States to brokers and dealers and to others for purchasing or carrying securities, collected two or three times a year by the Board of Governors of the Federal Reserve System and the Comptroller of the Currency. The percentage change in such loans by the weekly reporting member banks of the Federal Reserve System is then applied to these inclusive figures to obtain a weekly estimate of security loans by all banks in the United States. As new inclusive statistics become available, the weekly estimates are revised for the period between the dates for which the inclusive data are available.

TABLE IV

ESTIMATED SECURITY LOANS OF ALL BANKS IN THE UNITED STATES
(Millions of Dollars)

End of Quarter	Year-End Total	Loans to Brokers and Dealers	Loans to Others
1939			
June		774	852
September		630	813
December	1,662	845	817
1940			
March		735	776
June		492	762
September		495	748
December	1,438	690	748
1941			
March		643	729
June		582	725
September		574	702
December	1,317	637	680
1942			
March		470	661
June		503	646
September		602	619
December	1,603	987	616
1943			
March		701	555
June		1148	685
September		2224	1613
December	2,353	1435	918
1944			
March		1667	1276
June		2328	2321
September		1715	1325
December	4,756	2392	2364
1945			
March		1857	1505
June		3157	3562
September		2711	2102
December	6,806	3188	3618
1946			
March		3293	3056
June		2538	2737
September		1735	2133
December	3,493	1771	1722

TABLE IV *(Cont'd.)*

End of Quarter	Year-End Total	Loans to Brokers and dealers	Loans to Others
1947			
March		898	1343
June		1562	1311
September		1066	1331
December	2,076	831	1245
1948			
March		940	1073
June		1189	1131
September		1117	1049
December	2,439	1444	995
1949			
March		1644	922
June		2057	952
September		1818	937
December	2,706	1810	896
1950			
March		1829	863
June		1840	958
September		1607	1051
December	2,961	1890	1071
1951			
March		1692	1045
June		1614	1050
September		1332	997
December	2,636	1634	1002
1952			
March		1240	951
June		2200	928
September		1315	1096
December	3,188	2060	1128
1953			
March		1579	1125
June		1595	1087
September		1821	1046
December	3,618	2387	1231
1954			
March		1907	1219
June		2462	1283
September		2521	1320
December	4,557	2999	1558
1955			
March		2639	1550
June		2886	1657
September		2577	1686
December	5,072	3271	1801

TABLE IV *(Cont'd.)*

End of Quarter	Year-End Total	Loans to Brokers and dealers	Loans to Others
1956			
March		2712	1844
June		2727	1779
September		2394	1735
December	4,373	2638	1735
1957			
March		1993	1655
June		2197	1657
September		2087	1578
December	4,250	2601	1649
1958			
March		2471	1820
June		3784	1956
September		1973	1785
December	4,698	2832	1866
1959			
March		2032	1978
June		2163	1946
September		2213	1865
December	4,602	2769	1833

The statistical series of borrowings by members of the New York Stock Exchange is otherwise more limited in coverage, since it leaves out borrowings by security houses that are not members of the Exchange and by other classes of borrowers.

The New York Stock Exchange has published this series, shown on Chart VII, for the period since September, 1918, except for December, 1922 through December, 1926.

3. *Net debit balances of customers* of New York Stock Exchange member firms, published by the New York Stock Exchange since November, 1931. These debit balances of customers have given rise in recent years to the larger part of the borrowings by member firms of the New York Stock Exchange, and hence of bank loans to security brokers and dealers.

In appraising the volume of security credit in use at any one time, it is essential to select from the available series the statistics that are suited to the particular comparisons being made.

Chart VII

NEW YORK STOCK EXCHANGE MEMBER BORROWINGS *
1918–1959

End of Year **

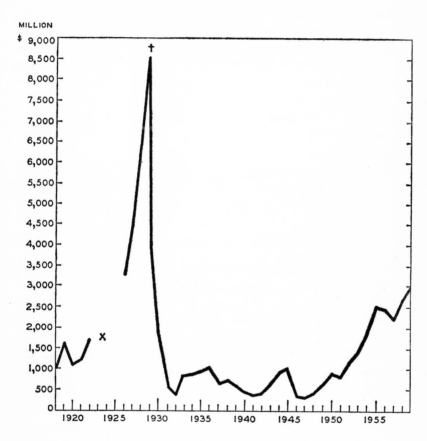

* Including borrowings on U. S. Government securities.
✕ 1923, 1924 and 1925 not available.
† September 1929. ** Last Wednesday since 1955.
SOURCE: New York Stock Exchange.

61

Historical Comparisons

Historical comparisons of security loans outstanding should include the period of the later 1920's, when security credit expanded to unprecedented proportions.

The statistical series of brokers' loans best adapted for such comparisons is that of New York Stock Exchange member borrowings, which goes back to 1918. It includes loans obtained from non-bank lenders and provides a consistent record of the volume of credit used by these borrowers for purchasing and carrying securities. Chart VII shows that such loans have never again even approached the very high level they attained in the late 1920's, despite the great subsequent growth of the economy.

Other series of security credit statistics, such as security loans made by member banks of the Federal Reserve System, indicate a similar pattern. Historical comparisons of bank security loan data over a longer period are not feasible. Until 1938, these data embraced all loans on stock and bond collateral, whereas beginning with that year only loans *to purchase and carry securities* have been included.

Historical comparisons thus demonstrate that the volume of security credit in use has remained far below the level reached in the late 1920's, in sharp contrast with the great expansion in the use of credit generally that has occurred since that time.

Security Loans and Private Debt

Security credit is one segment of private debt. Chart VIII traces the ratio of security credit, as measured by security loans made by banks to brokers and dealers and to others, to all outstanding private debt for the period since 1939. Security loans have constituted approximately 1% of total private debt during this period of rapid expansion of private indebtedness due to economic growth and inflation, except for the years 1944-46 when loans on Government securities expanded sharply in connection with war financing. At the end of 1929, security loans by banks, which included "non-purpose" loans at that time, were 7% of all private debt outstanding. Allowance must be made for

Chart VIII
RATIO OF SECURITY CREDIT * TO ALL PRIVATE DEBT
1939–1959

End of Year

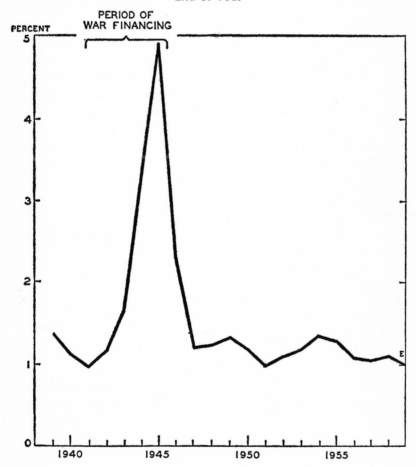

* Including credit advanced by Canadian bank agencies. E = estimate.

SOURCES: New York Stock Exchange; *Survey of Current Business,* Sept. 1953, May 1957, May 1959; *Statement of Assets and Liabilities of the Chartered Banks of Canada; Canada Year Book,* 1940, p. 817; 1945, p. 1005; 1947, p. 994.

this broader coverage of bank security loan statistics in 1929 in making comparisons with the ratios for the years since 1939. For a brief period at the peak of the boom in 1929, the ratio of all security collateral loans to private debt was over 10%.

Security loans comprise two major types of credit, as discussed in Chapter II. Loans to investors and speculators to purchase and carry securities or "customer credit," [2] which is the larger part of the total, constitutes a form of personal debt comparable with consumer and home mortgage debt. Loans to security brokers and dealers to finance their activities constitute credit advanced to the security business and are comparable with commercial loans of banks. To the extent that brokers and dealers borrow to finance the debit balances of their customers, there is a large element of overlapping in these two series of security loan statistics.

The increase in customer security credit, including debit balances of customers of New York Stock Exchange firms and security loans by banks to others than brokers and dealers in securities, is compared in Chart IX with the rise in consumer and home mortgage debt since 1939. The chart shows that security credit has lagged far behind other forms of personal credit in the era of rapid economic expansion of the past two decades.

Loans to brokers and dealers in securities, to finance both their customers and their own underwriting and inventories, have constituted a slight proportion of total business debt, corporate and non-corporate, as can be seen in Chart X. Only in 3 of the 21 years (excluding 1943-1946, the period of war finance, when borrowing on U. S. Government securities accounted for a large proportion of the total) have security loans to brokers and dealers accounted for as much as 1% of business debt outstanding.

Security Loans and Total Bank Loans

Bank loans for purchasing and carrying securities are a segment of bank lending. Their relative magnitude is at times

---

[2] "Customer credit," as reported monthly in the *Federal Reserve Bulletin*, includes net debit balances with New York Stock Exchange firms carrying margin accounts and loans to others than brokers and dealers for purchasing and carrying securities by reporting member banks.

Chart IX

GROWTH OF SECURITY, CONSUMER AND MORTGAGE CREDIT
1939–1959

End of Year

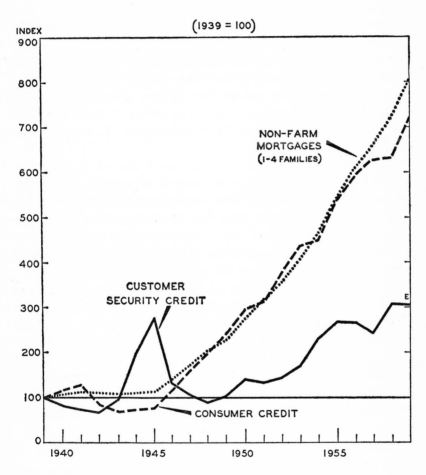

$(1939 = 100)$

INDEX

NON-FARM MORTGAGES (1-4 FAMILIES)

CUSTOMER SECURITY CREDIT

CONSUMER CREDIT

E = estimate.

SOURCES: New York Stock Exchange; *Federal Reserve Bulletin; Survey of Current Business,* Sept. 1953, May 1957, May 1959.

significant for the conduct of credit control and monetary policy.

The ratio of bank loans to purchase and carry securities to total bank loans outstanding since 1926 is traced on Chart XI. As already stated, statistics for bank loans on security collateral until 1938 included loans for business and consumption purposes, and so are not fully comparable with the later statistics.

Security loans, it is evident from the chart, have accounted for a small fraction of bank loans since 1947. The sharp rise in the ratio in 1944-45 was due to lending on Government securities issued to finance the huge Treasury deficit of World War II. This segment of bank credit has lagged far behind the great increase in bank lending that has accompanied the growth of the economy since the end of World War II. Chart XI shows that security loans could not have been a significant factor in the decision of the Federal Reserve authorities to apply over-all restrictive credit policies on a number of occasions since the end of World War II to restrain expansion of bank lending.

The above charts make clear that the volume of security credit in use in recent years has not been large enough to affect quantitative credit control materially. There has been nothing like the sharp rise in such lending that occurred in 1928-29.

Ratio of Security Borrowings to Security Values

Although not directly related to credit control, the effect of security loans on the level of stock prices is of interest.

One measure of the effect of security loans on the level of stock prices is the ratio of such borrowings to the market value of outstanding stocks. If security loans are relatively high in relation to the aggregate value of stocks, it could be assumed that such borrowings have influenced and will continue to influence the level of stock prices to a substantial degree.

Security credit influences the market price level chiefly through customer borrowings to purchase and carry securities. The bulk of such borrowings are incurred to carry stocks listed on the New York Stock Exchange. Hence, one measure of how security credit affects the level of stock prices is the ratio of customers' net debit

Chart X

RATIO OF BROKERS' LOANS TO BUSINESS DEBT *
1939–1959

End of Year

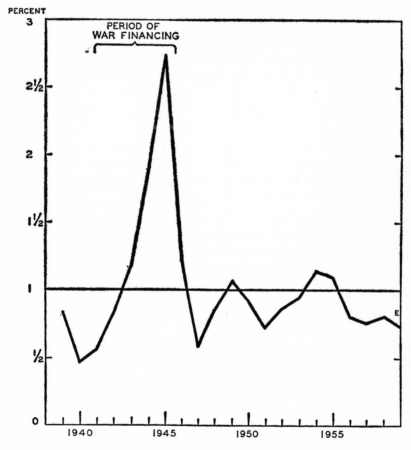

* Ratio of loans to brokers and dealers by all active banks to all private debt except farm, consumer and residential mortgage. E = estimate.

SOURCES: *Annual Reports of the Comptroller of the Currency; Survey of Current Business,* Sept. 1953, May 1957, May 1959.

Chart XI

RATIO OF BANK SECURITY LOANS TO TOTAL BANK LOANS
1926–1959 *

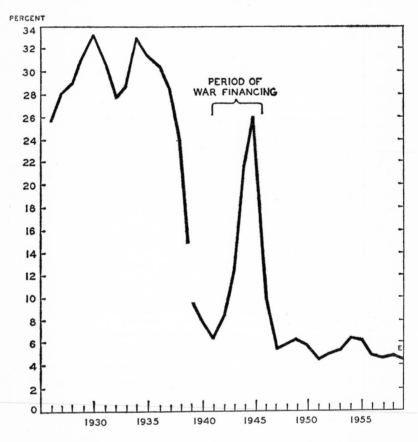

* 1926-1938, end of June; 1939-1959, end of year. Since 1939 excludes non-purpose loans. E = estimate.

SOURCES: New York Stock Exchange; *Annual Reports of the Comptroller of the Currency; Monetary and Banking Statistics; Federal Reserve Bulletin.*

68

balances as reported by member firms of the New York Stock Exchange to the value of stocks listed on the Exchange.[3] Chart XII shows this ratio has been less than 2% throughout the two decades 1939-59.

Commercial bank security loans to others than brokers and dealers are also made in considerable but indeterminate part to carry securities listed on the New York Stock Exchange. Chart XIII shows the ratio of customer borrowings from both member firms of the New York Stock Exchange and commercial banks to the value of stocks listed on the Exchange during the same 21-year period. The ratio is overstated to the extent that loans to carry securities other than stocks listed on the Exchange are included in the total of customer security credit.

The Securities and Exchange Commission estimated the value of all publicly held stocks owned by individuals, including personal trusts and non-profit corporations, at $248 billion at the end of 1957 and $355 billion at the end of 1958. The ratio of security loans made by all U. S. banks and foreign bank agencies to these totals was 1.7% at the end of 1957 and 1.3% at the end of 1958.

These ratios are so low as to demonstrate that security credit extension could not have influenced the level of stock prices to any substantial extent during this 20-year period.

Change in Security Loans and the Level of Stock Prices

There is a possibility that security credit, even though constituting a low ratio of the value of listed stocks, exerts a disproportionate effect on the level of stock prices as a marginal market factor. The relation between security loan *changes* and *changes* in the market price of listed stocks throws light on this possibility.

Changes in customer credit, including bank security loans to others than brokers and dealers that include loans on securities

---

[3] Debit balances may be increased also by purchases of securities other than stocks listed on the New York Stock Exchange, so that this ratio is actually lower than the figures indicate. On the other hand, excluding institutional holdings from the total market value of listed stocks would raise the ratio. Unfortunately, data on institutional holdings are not available for a continuous series.

Chart XII

RATIO OF CUSTOMERS' NET DEBIT BALANCES
TO THE MARKET VALUE OF STOCKS LISTED
ON THE NEW YORK STOCK EXCHANGE
1939–1959

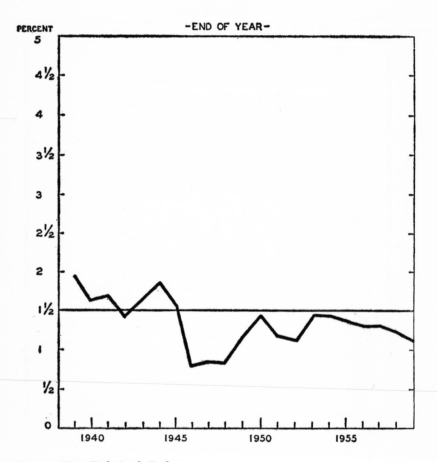

SOURCE: New York Stock Exchange.

Chart XIII

RATIO OF CUSTOMER SECURITY LOANS *
TO THE MARKET VALUE OF STOCKS LISTED
ON THE NEW YORK STOCK EXCHANGE
1939–1959

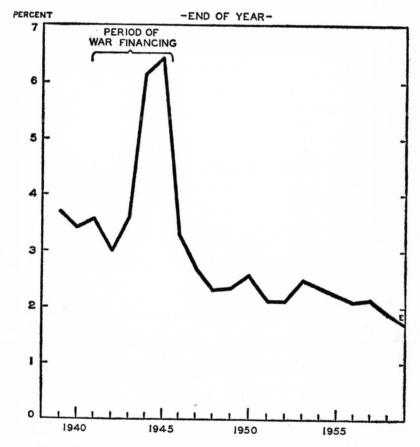

* Customers' net debit balances of N.Y.S.E. member firms plus all bank security loans to others than brokers and dealers. E = estimate.

SOURCES: New York Stock Exchange; *Annual Reports of the Comptroller of the Currency.*

other than listed stocks, are compared in Table V with changes in Standard and Poor's index of prices of 500 listed common stocks for the period since 1946. Comparisons for the preceding years are distorted by the bulge in security loans incident to Treasury offerings to finance the war.

TABLE V

CHANGE IN CUSTOMER SECURITY LOANS AND IN STOCK PRICES
1947-1959

Year	Change in Customer Security Loans		Change in Common Stock Prices (Standard & Poor's Index—1941-43 = 10)	
	(in Millions of Dollars)	(%)	(Index)	(%)
1947	−447	−19.7	0.00	0.0
1948	−277	−15.2	−0.10	− 0.7
1949	+231	+14.9	+1.56	+10.3
1950	+652	+36.7	+3.65	+21.8
1951	−134	− 5.5	+3.36	+16.5
1952	+199	+ 8.7	+2.80	+11.8
1953	+573	+23.0.	−1.76	− 6.6
1954	+1,060	+36.2	+11.17	+45.0
1955	+639	+16.0	+9.50	+26.4
1956	− 35	− 0.8	+1.19	+ 2.6
1957	−392	− 8.5	−6.68	−14.3
1958	+1,098	+26.1	+15.22	+38.1
1959	− 34	− 0.6	+4.68	+ 8.5

Changes in customer security loans were in the same direction as changes in value of listed stocks in 8 of the 13 years. Changes in the amount of security loans were sufficient to have had some influence upon the trend of prices in 4 of these years, a comparison of security loan with stock price changes indicates.

Loans Secured by U. S. Government Securities

A varying, but at times material, proportion of security loans outstanding since 1939 has been secured by U. S. Government obligations.[4]

Government securities may be pledged as collateral because

---

[4] See *Treasury-Federal Reserve Study of the Government Securities Market,* 1959. Part I, pp. 30 ff.

larger amounts can be borrowed on them and interest rates are often lower, even if the loan is for the purpose of buying other securities. But most loans secured by Treasury obligations are for the purpose of purchasing or carrying such issues.

The proportion of outstanding security loans against U. S. Government obligations increases quite sharply when there is increased public interest in buying and holding Government securities, especially as new financing is undertaken by the Treasury at such times. At other times, the proportion may fall to a low level. This was illustrated by the sharp rise in the proportion of security loans on U. S. Government issues late in 1957 and during the first half of 1958.

At the end of June, 1957, only a little over 1% of the "customer credit" extended on securities was secured by U. S. Government issues. At the end of June, 1958, when public interest in purchasing Treasury issues was strong, the ratio was over 7%, but it had fallen back to 4% by the end of that year.

Of the money borrowed by brokers and dealers, a little more than 2% was secured by U. S. Government securities at the end of June, 1957, but over 19% was so secured at the end of June, 1958, and less than 10% at the end of 1958. A large part of the credit used by security dealers to carry inventories of U. S. Government securities was obtained through repurchase agreements, rather than loans. Hence, the ratios given understate the proportion of total credit utilized by brokers and dealers that was backed by U. S. Government obligations.

SUMMARY

The magnitude of security credit can be measured by several series of statistics of such lending issued by bank supervisory authorities and the New York Stock Exchange. The most inclusive available measure is that of all bank loans to purchase and carry securities, as estimated by the Department of Research and Statistics of the Stock Exchange.

Security loans have consistently remained quite small in aggregate amount by comparison with the volume reached for a time in the late 1920's. This contrasts strikingly with the vast expansion of credit use in virtually every other segment of the economy that has accompanied economic growth and inflation since the end of World War II.

Loans to purchase or carry securities have constituted only about 1% of total private debt and a little over 4% of all bank loans in recent years. Since 1939, the rise in security loans has been quite modest by comparison with the very rapid and persistent expansion of consumer and home mortgage debt. Loans to security brokers and dealers have rarely accounted for as much as 1% of all business borrowings.

Since security loans have not increased materially, they do not share responsibility for the enormous credit expansion of the past decade and the consequent resort at times to drastic over-all credit restriction by the Federal Reserve authorities.

Security credit expansion has not again interfered with the effectiveness of quantitative credit control, as it did in 1928-29. Therefore, it has not been a factor in the adoption of restrictive over-all credit policies during the post-war period. Credit restriction has been adopted, rather, because of too rapid expansion of business and personal borrowing.

Security credit, as contrasted with other personal and business credit, has thus been performing its economic functions without requiring a vast expansion of the dollar volume of such credit outstanding.

Chapter 7

REGULATION OF SECURITY CREDIT BEFORE 1934

Proposals to regulate security credit were advanced long before the enactment of the Securities Exchange Act in 1934.

Regulation of security loans was first proposed during and after the money panics that occurred periodically before the establishment of the Federal Reserve System. This was particularly true following the panic of 1907, when a committee appointed by Governor Hughes of New York to investigate trading in securities and commodities suggested that the New York Stock Exchange have member firms require a minimum margin of 20% on transactions. The Congressional committee which conducted the Money Trust Investigation in 1912, the so-called Pujo Committee, made a similar recommendation.

The object of this proposal in each case was not to limit the use of credit in the security markets. Rather, it was to protect speculators from their own imprudence, and so by implication to contribute to greater stability of security prices.

The New York Stock Exchange Resolution of 1913

The New York Stock Exchange adopted the principle of a minimum requirement, and thereby took the first concrete step towards regulation of the use of security credit, when it passed the following resolution on February 13, 1913:

> That the acceptance and carrying of an account for a customer, either a member or a nonmember, without proper and adequate margin may constitute an act detrimental to the welfare and interest of the exchange, and the offending member may be proceeded against under Section 8 of Article 7 of the Constitution.[1]

---

[1] This section imposed a penalty of suspension up to one year.

Under this resolution, minimum margins of 20% of debit balances during most of the 1920's, and 25% after June, 1929, came to be regarded as an unwritten rule for Exchange members. Individual firms maintained substantially higher margin requirements, especially during 1928 and 1929, and to that extent tended to prevent an even greater rise in security loans than actually occurred at that time.[2]

These minimum margin requirements were not intended to regulate security price movements or to protect investors, as was envisaged in the Hughes investigation. Rather, the protection of the solvency of Exchange members by lessening the risk of loss from undermargined accounts was the major consideration.

A second, quite indirect, early approach to the regulation of security credit was the provision of the Federal Reserve Act barring security collateral loans by member banks from rediscount privileges at the Federal Reserve banks. This was designed both to make security loans a less desirable banking asset and to prevent the use of Federal Reserve credit by member banks to expand their loans on securities. However, member banks could obtain additional reserves when needed by rediscounting eligible paper at their Federal Reserve banks, and could then use these reserves to support an expansion of security loans if they wished. The use made of additional reserve credit by the banking system is not affected by the way in which this credit is obtained by member banks in the first place. Hence, inability to rediscount security loans has had little effect upon the volume of such lending by banks.

---

[2] One New York Stock Exchange member firm sent the following statement to its clients in October, 1928:

"It is generally recognized that conditions influencing security market movements are such at the present time that a higher degree of protection on accounts is necessary. Many banks are requiring larger margins on collateral loans as well as decreasing materially the figures at which they accept stocks, and many Stock Exchange houses are stiffening their margin requirements as they properly should for the better protection of their clients and themselves.

Therefore, our requirements will be as follows:

Securities selling below $10, cash only; from $10 to $20, 50 per cent; $20 to $30, 10 points; above $30, 30 per cent of the purchase price. . . .

No margin accounts will be opened on an initial deposit of less than $1,000."

The World War I Control Experience

World War I witnessed a third and far more ambitious and effective experiment in security loan regulation.

The entrance of the United States into the war in April, 1917, was followed by withdrawals of funds from the call loan market by banks, both to buy Government securities and to make loans on Government obligations bought by their customers. Banks also preferred to acquire eligible paper for possible future rediscounting needs. The resulting shortage of funds for loans on securities other than Government obligations threatened to disrupt the stock market, and it was feared that falling stock prices would impede future Treasury financing.

To assure the security markets of a reasonable supply of credit for their needs, a Subcommittee on Money Rates of the Liberty Loan Committee was appointed. It was composed of Governor Benjamin Strong of the Federal Reserve Bank of New York as chairman and the presidents of eight of the leading New York City banks. This group, called the Money Committee, undertook to assure that the $450 million then being loaned on call by New York banks for their own account would continue to be made available for security loans on stocks and bonds other than Government obligations. Each of 63 banks in New York City was assigned a loan quota based on its assets. An additional $200 million was to be kept available for time loans on securities. A money desk was established on the floor of the New York Stock Exchange at that time to allot available loanable funds equitably among member firms at set rates of interest.

To implement this plan and assure that participating banks would meet their lending quotas, daily reports on brokers' loans were collected by the Federal Reserve Bank of New York beginning in October, 1917. These reports were held confidential, and the figures were not published until some time after the war, although the data continued to be collected after the Money Committee was dissolved.

In August, 1918, when the approaching end of the war stimulated public buying of stocks, it was feared that heavy borrowing to carry stocks on margin would cut into bank and individual subscriptions to new Treasury security offerings. The Money Committee then shifted its objective to limiting the volume of stock market loans. Governor Strong, as chairman, wrote to the president of the New York Stock Exchange asking its cooperation in holding the volume of security loans to the amount then outstanding. To implement this effort, the Governing Committee of the Exchange was asked to collect daily reports of demand and time borrowings of each Stock Exchange member firm for the confidential use of the Money Committee. These reports were used to check on any increase in borrowings by individual member firms. With this same end in view, minimum margin requirements on security loans were raised by New York City banks by joint agreement at the Committee's request to 30% on mixed rail and industrial stocks and to 37½% on unmixed collateral. The Money Committee also asked that time loans on securities be limited to shorter periods.[3]

The stated objective of the Money Committee was solely to protect Treasury war financing from the adverse effect of either a severe shortage of security loans or excessive demands for such funds to finance public purchases of securities on the stock exchange. This implied that once the financing of the war was completed, control over security lending would be ended. The Money Committee terminated its activities in January, 1919, following the war's end, because of the then prevailing view that special controls over security loans were not required once the emergency created by war financing of the Government had passed.

The wartime experience showed that security lending could be regulated by selective controls. The principals later expressed differing views on the termination of wartime control over security loans. Governor Benjamin Strong testified in 1921 before the Joint Commission of Agricultural Inquiry of Congress:

---

[3] B. H. Beckhart, *The New York Money Market*, (New York: Columbia University Press, 1932), Vol. III, Chap. III; and testimony of Governor Benjamin Strong in Hearings before the *Joint Commission of Agricultural Inquiry*, 67th Congress, First Session, (Washington: Government Printing Office, 1921).

> My own belief at the time, personally, and my belief at this
> time is that had it been possible for us to have continued that
> type of arbitrary control, it would have been a good thing to do
> it. It was one of the controls . . . which was exceedingly effec-
> tive and beneficial.

Yet in the middle 1920's, Governor Strong expressed a strong
distaste for direct control by the Federal Reserve System over
bank lending to limit security loans.

Russell C. Leffingwell, as Assistant Secretary of the Treasury,
wrote even before the discontinuation of the Committee:

> It is the earnest hope of the Treasury that, growing out of the
> very salutary action of the Money Subcommittee and of the
> Stock Exchange authorities during the period of the war . . .
> there may be evolved some plan for preventing the recurrence,
> after the restoration of peace conditions, of those erratic and
> violent fluctuations in rates for call money and those feverish
> movements of prices on the Stock Exchange which in the past
> have been of great concern to the judicious.

President H. G. S. Noble of the New York Stock Exchange
had expressed, in 1919, the view which prevailed:

> The present restrictions on security loans have largely killed
> the buying power of the market. . . . Any bad news coming
> upon us suddenly and precipitating liquidation would find the
> market thin and vulnerable and open to the danger of serious
> demoralization.[4]

A lasting result of the World War I control experience was
the compilation of statistics of security loans. However, regular
publication of such statistics was not begun until 1926, when
the Federal Reserve Board began publishing weekly data on
loans to brokers by New York City reporting member banks in
the hope that publication of the statistics would help restrain
expansion of such credit. The New York Stock Exchange, under
a resolution adopted by its Governing Committee, started regular
publication of monthly figures for borrowings by its members
in New York City at the same time.

---

[4] Lester V. Chandler, *Benjamin Strong, Central Banker*, (Washington: Brookings Institution, 1958), pp. 129-137 and 427-431.

Reliance on General Credit Control

A fourth regulatory approach, used in 1919-1920 and again in 1928-29, was to curb security loan expansion by means of general credit control measures, including sales of Government securities in the open market by the Federal Reserve banks and higher rediscount rates.

In each instance, an over-all tight money policy by the Federal Reserve System *finally* checked the expansion of security loans and brought about a contraction. However, this occurred *only after* a considerable lapse of time during which large amounts of additional funds were loaned on securities, because borrowers were ready to pay high interest rates to secure funds to finance purchases of stocks in a rapidly rising market.

The New York Stock Exchange Rule

The New York Stock Exchange tightened its control over the grant of credit by its members when the Governing Committee on August 2, 1933 adopted a rule authorizing the Committee on Business Conduct to "fix the minimum amount of margin which . . . members or firms must require on existing margin accounts." The committee then set 30% of the debit balance as the minimum margin to be maintained on accounts having a debit balance of more than $5,000 and 50% where the debit balance was $5,000 or less.[5] It was specified that "substantial additional margin must be required in all cases where the securities carried are subject to sudden changes in value or where the amount of any particular security carried is unusual." Moreover, the Committee on Business Conduct, in analyzing answers to the financial questionnaires that were first distributed in 1922, charged members' capital for amounts by which customers' accounts were under-margined.

The objective of the New York Stock Exchange in adopting these minimum margin rules was to safeguard the solvency of

---

[5] Since March 5, 1945, minimum margin requirement has been stated as a percentage of market value of securities in the account, and not of the debit balance.

Exchange members in the public interest, by maintaining reasonable margin protection at all times on customers' margin accounts. This carried further the principle embodied in the original resolution of the Exchange, adopted in 1913.

The Banking Act of 1933

The severe depression and deflation of the early 1930's gave rise to a series of Congressional investigations to determine and correct the causes of the economic difficulties of the time. Inquiries into the nation's financial system led to legislation that effected far-reaching changes in banking, mortgage financing and security issuance and trading.

Regulation of security credit was one of the subjects of intensive Congressional study. This was an inevitable result of the unprecedented expansion of security loans in the late 1920's, the inability of the Federal Reserve System quickly and fully to check this expansion by use of its over-all credit control powers, and the aftermath of large-scale forced liquidation of securities to meet margin calls in the early 1930's.

The first major effort to subject security loans to special controls was made in the Banking Act of 1933. This law was the result of a comprehensive study of the nation's banking system conducted by the Senate Committee on Banking and Currency under the guidance of Senator Carter Glass of Virginia, who had been a chief architect of the original Federal Reserve Act.

The Banking Act of 1933 includes provisions that give the Federal Reserve authorities power to limit the supply of funds for security loans in two ways. First, they are given power to limit the percentage of a member bank's capital and surplus that may be loaned on security collateral. Secondly, the Federal Reserve Board is authorized to suspend borrowing privileges at the Federal Reserve bank for member banks that increase their security loans to an extent that is deemed excessive.

Section 7 of the law goes furthest in giving the Federal Reserve Board power to control the supply of security loans. It provides:

> Upon the affirmative vote of not less than six of its members the Federal Reserve Board shall have power to fix from time to

time for each Federal Reserve district the percentage of individual bank capital and surplus which may be represented by
loans secured by stock or bond collateral made by member
banks within such district . . . and it shall be the duty of the
Board to establish such percentages with a view to preventing
the undue use of bank loans for the speculative carrying of securities.

Three provisions of the Banking Act of 1933 give the Federal
Reserve authorities power to limit security loans of member banks
by use of the threat of suspension of borrowing privileges from
Federal Reserve banks.

Section 3 authorizes the Federal Reserve Board to suspend
borrowing privileges of a member bank where "undue use is
being made of bank credit for the speculative carrying of or
trading in securities, real estate, or commodities." Section 7 gives
the Federal Reserve Board "power to direct any member bank
to refrain from further increase of its loans secured by stock or
bond collateral for any period up to one year under suspension
of all rediscount privileges at Federal Reserve banks." And Section 9 makes member banks ineligible for advances secured by
Government obligations from their Federal Reserve bank "if
they increase their loans on securities or loans to members of a
stock exchange or to security dealers" despite an official warning
of the reserve bank of the district or of the Federal Reserve
Board to the contrary.

These provisions of the Banking Act of 1933, designed to
regulate security lending by limiting the *supply* of loanable
funds from member banks of the Federal Reserve System, have
not been put to use. There has been no occasion even to consider
their use because, within one year after the passage of the
Banking Act of 1933, Congress enacted the Securities Exchange
Act of 1934 which provided for regulation of security credit
by limiting the *demand* for such loans through setting minimum
margin requirements. Since minimum margin requirements affect
broker as well as bank lending on securities, and since the
Federal Reserve authorities have regarded margin regulation
to be an adequate regulatory device to date, these provisions of
the Banking Act of 1933 have never been used.

The Banking Act of 1933 also makes it unlawful for member banks of the Federal Reserve System to act as agents for non-banking lenders in making security collateral loans to brokers or dealers. The New York Clearing House had already prohibited its member and nonmember clearing banks from making or servicing security loans for others than banks in November, 1931. This was designed to prevent a repetition of 1929's rapid expansion of loans to brokers "for the account of others," with the New York banks acting as agents.

Regulation of security credit under the Securities Exchange Act of 1934, the chief example of selective credit control in American financial history, is considered at length in the following chapters.

SUMMARY

Regulation of security credit was proposed or attempted from time to time, especially during and following periods of stringency or crisis, before the enactment of the Securities Exchange Act of 1934.

The several approaches to regulation proposed or tried between 1907 and 1934 were:

1. Establishment of a minimum margin requirement to protect speculators from their own imprudence. This was urged by the Hughes Committee in 1909 and the Money Trust Investigation of 1912.

2. Adoption by the New York Stock Exchange of its resolution of 1913 requiring "proper and adequate margin" from customers.

3. Prohibition of rediscounting of security collateral loans by the Federal Reserve banks in the Federal Reserve Act of 1913.

4. Rationing of security credit during World War I by a committee of bankers to keep available and distribute equitably a limited supply of such credit. The machinery thus set up was used to restrict security credit when the approaching end of the war expanded the demand for such loans. This experiment was regarded as an emergency measure to prevent interference with Government war borrowing, and so was terminated when the

financing of the war had been completed. However, it demonstrated that security credit could be regulated effectively by selective controls, and so influenced later thinking on this subject.

5. Reliance upon general credit restraint by the Federal Reserve System to limit security loans in 1919-20 and in 1928-29.

6. Establishment of a minimum margin requirement by the New York Stock Exchange in 1933 of 30% of debit balances, to safeguard stock exchange member firms.

7. The grant to the Federal Reserve authorities of powers to limit the volume of member bank security lending by the Banking Act of 1933. This law also prohibited member banks of the Federal Reserve System from making security collateral loans to brokers and dealers as agents for nonbanking lenders.

Chapter 8

REGULATION OF SECURITY CREDIT—
THE SECURITIES EXCHANGE ACT OF 1934

The economic events that followed the stock market crash of October, 1929, aroused widespread interest in the subject of security credit. Besides spawning a number of books on margin trading and brokers' loans,[1] these events revived discussion, such as had been carried on after the panic of 1907, of regulation of security loans. They also led to the Senate Investigation of Stock Exchange Practices, popularly known as the Pecora Investigation. Out of this investigation emerged the Securities Exchange Act of 1934 which, among other provisions, instituted direct Federal regulation of security credit for the first time.

Historical Background of the Act

Bills to regulate and restrict security loans began to appear in Congress shortly after the beginning of the depression. The half dozen such measures introduced between 1930 and 1934 proposed three types of regulation: taxation of margin trading, limitation of the volume of security loans made by banks, and outright prohibition of margin trading.

In March, 1930, Representative McCleod of Michigan introduced a bill to levy a tax of from 1 to 50 per cent on margin trading "in order to avoid in the future such unwholesome

---

[1] Among others: Fritz Machlup, *The Stock Market, Credit and Capital Formation* (London: 1940) (German edition: 1931); Lewis H. Haney and others, *Brokers' Loans* (New York: Harper and Brothers, 1932); Twentieth Century Fund, *Stock Market Control* (New York: 1934), and *The Security Markets* (New York: 1939).

reactions as that of 1929." In June, 1930, Senator Glass introduced an omnibus monetary reform bill that contained provisions restricting the volume of loans which national banks could advance to stock exchange members. In December, 1930, Senator Heflin of Alabama offered a bill prohibiting margin trading in brokerage accounts and limiting the rate on call loans by banks to 8 per cent.

These proposals failed to win support. The McCleod and Heflin bills never came to a vote. The Glass bill, after a long and tortuous legislative history, eventually formed the basis for the Banking Act of 1933,[2] which affected security lending to a limited degree.

As the depression deepened, more attention was given the subject of security credit regulation. The press gave publicity to recommendations by Melvin A. Traylor, president of the First National Bank of Chicago, to eliminate margin trading in accounts of less than $10,000, and by Federal Judge Clark to abolish all trading on margin.[3]

On March 2, 1932, the Senate authorized its Committee on Banking and Currency "to make a thorough and complete investigation of the practices with respect to the buying and selling and the borrowing and lending of listed securities upon the various stock exchanges . . ." The Committee began its hearings on April 11, 1932, and Ferdinand Pecora became counsel to the Committee on January 14, 1933.

Meanwhile, interest in the subject of security credit had become broad enough to make it something of an issue in the Presidential campaign of 1932. The Democratic party's platform included a plank calling for the regulation of stock exchanges and security credit and, in a campaign speech in August, Franklin D. Roosevelt advocated Federal regulation of stock market credit.

The Dickinson Report

In the Spring of 1933, shortly after Roosevelt's inauguration, Secretary of Commerce Roper, at the President's suggestion, formed a committee under the chairmanship of Assistant Secre-

---

[2] See Chapter 7.
[3] *New York Times,* May 9, 1931; June 24, 1931.

tary of Commerce John Dickinson[4] to study and report on Federal legislation to regulate security transactions and security exchanges. The Dickinson Report on the regulation of stock exchanges was issued on January 27, 1934. Its recommendations and attitude as regards regulation of security credit were extremely influential in the later drafting of the Securities Exchange Act.

The Dickinson Report stated:

> No attempt to deal with the abuses of stock exchange operations can omit the subject of margin trading. . . . The stock market vitally affects credit, which in turn directly affects commercial conditions. In part this is due to the practice of banks in making loans upon stock market collateral. . . .

The Dickinson Committee recommended that margin trading be restricted "within sound limits" in order to "curb excessive speculation." Its specific suggestions were:

1. that accounts should not be carried on margin unless the customer's equity was "at least a minimum amount in order to prevent the risking of savings by individuals who are unable to cope with the hazards of the market";

2. that margins of at least a stated percentage be required; and

3. that banks be required to confine their loans to brokers who observed the above requirements.

To administer and police the recommended regulations, the Committee suggested the establishment of a Federal Stock Exchange Authority either as a new agency or within the Federal Trade Commission. It also "suggested that the Federal Reserve Bank of any district, together with the Stock Exchange Authority, be empowered to prescribe margin requirements." The Committee conceded that margin requirements might impair the liquidity of securities. It contended, however, that "the social cost of liquidity has yet to be explored, and should be explored by the Federal Stock Exchange Authority."

The Dickinson Report constituted in effect the first chapter

---

[4] The other members of the Committee were A. A. Berle, Jr., Arthur H. Dean, James M. Landis, and Henry J. Richardson.

in the legislative history of the Securities Exchange Act. Events moved rapidly after its publication.

On February 3, Pecora expressed the opinion that "margin trading should be restricted or eliminated . . . if we would end this abuse of stock market gambling with the money of other people." This typified the extremist views frequently heard at this time.

On February 9, President Roosevelt sent a special message to Congress urging stock exchange regulation "for the protection of investors, for the safeguarding of values, and, so far as it may be possible, for the elimination of unnecessary, unwise, and destructive speculation."

Objectives of Proposed Margin Regulation [5]

On the day that the President sent his special message to Congress, Senator Duncan U. Fletcher of Florida and Representative Samuel Rayburn of Texas introduced in the Senate and in the House the "National Securities Exchange Act of 1934." Hearings on this bill clarified the purposes of its authors with reference to security credit regulation.

Thomas G. Corcoran told the Senate Banking Committee that two groups cooperated in writing the original draft of the Fletcher-Rayburn bill: "Mr. Pecora's group . . . and Mr. Landis' [James M. Landis of the Federal Trade Commission] group." Benjamin Cohen and Corcoran apparently drafted much of the bill. They consulted with members of Pecora's staff, including John T. Flynn and Pecora himself. On the provisions regulating security credit, they sought the advice of "the best men we could find to work on that matter in the Federal Reserve System." It has been reported that Winfield W. Riefler was consulted repeatedly on security credit regulation.

---

[5] The material in this section is derived from hearings and reports on stock exchange practices in the 73rd Congress, 2nd Session, 1934, namely: *Senate Report No. 1455*, "Stock Exchange Practices"; *Hearings before Committee on Banking and Currency, Part 15*, "Stock Exchange Practices"; *House Report No. 1383 and No. 1838*, "Stock Exchange Regulations"; *Hearings before House Committee on Interstate and Foreign Commerce*, "Stock Exchange Regulations." Also the *Congressional Record* and the *New York Times*, Feb.-June 1934.

According to Corcoran, "there was a very strong element that believed in cutting out margin trading altogether. This bill is a compromise between those who believe that you should eliminate margin trading altogether and those who are willing to go along with the stock exchange for a time in its thesis that a liquid market made liquid with borrowed funds is worth enough so that some margin money should be left in it, though not much." Despite this attitude, Senator Fletcher, in introducing the bill, claimed that "what is now put before the Congress is a moderate or middle-of-the-road program. The bill allows the use of ample credit in the conduct of stock exchanges."

The voluminous hearings on the Fletcher-Rayburn bill brought out a wide range of opinions concerning the purposes which margin regulation would serve.

Corcoran testified that there were two objectives of margin regulation: "One is to protect the lamb; another, and probably the more important of the two, although it does not appeal to one's human instincts as completely, is the protection of the national business system from the fluctuations that are induced by fluctuations in the market, which in turn stem back to the very exquisite liquidity you get when you have a lot of borrowed money in the market."

In addition to protecting the small trader and lessening the stock market's liquidity in order to limit price fluctuations, witnesses favoring the margin regulation provisions stressed as objectives a lessening of speculative activity in the stock market, prevention of a crash like that of 1929, and the protection of business and agricultural borrowers from a shortage of loanable funds and high interest rates resulting from a major expansion of brokers' loans.

The Congressional Committee Reports

The final reports on the Fletcher-Rayburn bill reflected diverse views of what should or would be achieved by security credit regulation.

The Report of the Senate Committee on Banking and Currency on the bill argued that "speculation in securities with borrowed money" was an important factor causing "the excessive and unrestrained speculation which has dominated the securities markets in recent years." It was critical of a high level of brokers' loans because "in the event of unfavorable developments in the financial world, such loans are promptly called," causing a collapse in security prices that "demoralized the margin trader." The report to the Senate argued further that "a rapid rise in stock prices, facilitated by brokers' borrowings, tends to make industry overoptimistic, to overstimulate production and to encourage the issuance of new and unnecessary securities." It also asserted that a main objective of margin regulation was "to protect the margin purchaser by making it impossible for him to buy securities on too thin a margin."

The Rayburn Report to the House was far more restrained and objective in its claims of what margin control could accomplish. "Without adequate control," the report said, "the too strong attraction of a speculative stock market for credit prevents a balanced utilization of the nation's credit resources in commerce, industry, and agriculture."

Holding that the primary purpose of margin regulation was to make possible a limitation of the total volume of stock market loans to assure adequate credit for commerce and industry, the final report to the House said:

> The main purpose of the margin provisions . . . is not to increase the safety of security loans, for lenders, banks and brokers, normally require sufficient collateral to make themselves safe. . . . Nor is the main purpose even protection of the small speculator . . . although such a result will be achieved as a by-product. . . . The main purpose is to give a Government credit agency an effective method of reducing the aggregate amount of the nation's credit resources which can be directed into the stock market and out of the other more desirable uses of commerce and industry . . . to prevent a recurrence of the pre-crash situation where funds which would otherwise have been available at normal interest rates for uses of local commerce, industry, and agriculture were drained by far higher rates into security loans and the New York call market.

The record thus indicates that exaggerated expectations of what security loan regulation would do for the investor, the stock market and the economy as a whole were entertained by authors and proponents of the bill and by the Senate Banking and Currency Committee in its final report on the measure. A more realistic and limited view of what margin regulation would do was reflected in the final report by the House Committee on Interstate and Foreign Commerce.

Later Legislative History of the Act

In the area of security credit control, the original Fletcher-Rayburn bill:

1. made it illegal for any member of a national securities exchange or "any person" who transacts a business in securities through the medium of any such member to lend on a security not registered on a national exchange;

2. set the maximum loan value on a security at 80 per cent of its lowest price during the preceding three years or 40 per cent of the current market, whichever was the higher, and this maximum loan value was to apply throughout the life of the loan;

3. vested the administration of the Act in the Federal Trade Commission;

4. empowered the FTC to lower but not to raise the loan value set in the original Act;

5. prohibited members of a national exchange or persons transacting a securities business through such a member from borrowing on securities from any person other than a member bank of the Federal Reserve System;

6. prohibited a member of an exchange from borrowing in excess of 1,000 per cent of his net current assets.

Opposition to the Original Bill

Immediately after its introduction, the bill ran into heavy weather. It was criticized both by those who favored the spirit and general principle of the legislation and by those who opposed it. And most of the barrage of criticism was directed at the credit provisions of the bill.

The *New York Times* reported that stock brokers were strongly opposed to the margin requirements of the bill. The brokers insisted that adequate control of security credit was provided by the bill's section limiting total borrowing by an exchange member and by the Banking Act of 1933 provisions giving the Federal Reserve Board powers to limit security lending by banks.[6]

Early in the hearings, spokesmen for investment bankers, the stock exchanges, the National Association of Manufacturers, the U. S. Chamber of Commerce and the financial press expressed opposition to the proposed measure. Among others, Richard Whitney, then president of the New York Stock Exchange, contended that sufficient authority existed in the Federal Reserve Act and the Banking Act of 1933 to prevent the abuses that the Fletcher-Rayburn bill proposed to curb, and that the margin requirements set in that bill would "impair, if not entirely destroy" the liquidity of the securities market. Sharp criticism was levelled at other credit provisions of the bill, such as the prohibition of loans on unregistered securities which, it was claimed, would cause hardship to small companies whose securities were not listed.

In April, the stock exchanges expressed concretely their opposition to the Fletcher-Rayburn bill by suggesting a substitute measure. This substitute's brief section on security loans was as follows:

> It shall be unlawful for any member of a national stock exchange or any broker or dealer transacting a business in securities through any such member, directly or indirectly, to extend or maintain credit to or for any person or to borrow any money, the repayment of which is secured by the pledge or hypothecation of any security, in contravention of such rules as may be established from time to time by the Federal Reserve Board for the purpose of preventing the excessive use of credit for speculation.[7]

This substitute proposal by the stock exchanges foreshadowed the form of regulation that was actually adopted, since it gave a broad grant of regulatory authority over security credit to the Federal Reserve Board.

Sympathetic and even enthusiastic advocates of Government regulation of security credit agreed with many of the criticisms

---

[6] *New York Times,* Feb. 25, 1934.
[7] *New York Times,* April 5, 1934.

of the original Fletcher-Rayburn bill. Dr. E. A. Goldenweiser thought the bill would have a decidedly deflationary effect, and so would be quite harmful in view of the depressed condition of the economy. He suggested that margin requirements apply to future security loans only, and then only at the time the loan was made and not for its life. Assistant Secretary of Commerce Dickinson thought that the bill placed too much power in the FTC and not enough in the Federal Reserve Board. He also believed that the margin requirements specified would be much too deflationary, since they would lead to a liquidation of perhaps $1 billion in security loans.

Dr. Alfred Bernheim, representing the Twentieth Century Fund which had just completed an exhaustive study of the securities markets, was especially critical of the bill's margin provisions. He pointed out that to prohibit loans on unregistered securities would disqualify state and municipal bonds as collateral, and the exclusion would encourage "bootleg" loans. Although the Twentieth Century Fund had criticized margin trading as making possible "excessive speculation," it was most unhappy with the bill's margin sections. "I believe," said Bernheim, "that the principle of relating collateral loans solely to market values is essentially unsound. . . . This method permits a pyramiding process—higher loans as prices are rising and accelerates liquidation when prices are dropping."

The Twentieth Century Fund proposed as a substitute that loan values on securities be fixed on the basis of earnings instead of market price. It suggested that the maximum loan value on stocks be twice the aggregate net earnings per share for the five years preceding the date of the loan, but in no case more than 60 per cent of the current market price. On bonds, it was suggested that the maximum loan be 80 per cent of the face or market value, whichever was lower. Although it was not adopted, the Fund's suggestion received considerable attention. Indeed, at one time the Fletcher-Rayburn bill contained a provision instructing the Federal Reserve Board and the Federal Trade Commission "to study the feasibility of fixing maximum loan values on the basis of earnings."

Revision of the Margin Provisions

The criticism of the original bill proved effective. The measure was taken out of committee and its credit provisions were thoroughly rewritten along lines suggested by the Federal Reserve Board and the Treasury. A revised bill was then turned over to the two Congressional Committees in mid-March of 1934.

The credit provisions of the rewritten bill were as follows:

1. The Federal Reserve Board was authorized to administer margin requirements.

2. Maximum loan values were not to exceed 40% of the current market price or 100% of the lowest market price during the preceding three years or since July 1, 1933, but not more than 75% of current market.

3. Margin requirements would not apply to loans outstanding on the date of the law's enactment until January 31, 1939.

4. The Federal Reserve Board was given the power to change margin requirements in "an emergency."

5. Undermargined accounts where the maximum initial loan under the bill's provisions would be 75% of the current market price could be continued so long as the loan did not exceed 85% of the current market price. Similarly, undermargined accounts where the initial maximum loan would be 40% could be continued if the loan did not exceed 60% of the current market price.

6. Margin provisions would not apply to "exempted securities," consisting of Government and Government-guaranteed obligations.

Final Changes and Enactment

Spokesmen for the stock exchanges and the investment bankers found the amended bill more to their liking. Most of the other critics were pleased with the changes that had been made. Nevertheless, in the Senate and House Committees the amended bill was subjected to additional amendments and additional redrafting.

The Senate Banking Committee adopted two very important

amendments proposed by Senator Glass: one replaced the Federal Trade Commission with a special Securities Exchange Commission as the administrative agency for the provisions other than credit regulation; the other eliminated fixed margin requirements and instead gave the Federal Reserve Board discretionary authority to regulate margins. Later, the Senate Committee voted to give the new SEC authority to regulate brokers' margins for customers, but to give the Federal Reserve Board the power to set margin requirements for security loans by member banks. The Senate Committee also fixed June 30, 1936 as the effective date for margin requirements on existing loans. After the Committee reported the bill to the Senate, Senator Bulkley of Ohio, a member of the Committee, proposed an amendment to prohibit all margin trading. Although it had the support of Senators Glass and Norris of Nebraska, this amendment was defeated, 48-30.

Meanwhile, the House Committee also had been busy amending its bill. When it was finally introduced on the floor,[8] its margin provisions differed from those in the Senate bill in three important respects. The House bill fixed the maximum loan limit at 55% of the current market price or 100% of the lowest price during the previous three years (or since January 1, 1933) but in any event no more than 75% of the current market price. More important, the Federal Reserve Board was given the power to raise or lower margin requirements, although the Federal Trade Commission remained responsible for administration of these requirements. Existing security loans were not to be subject to margin requirements until January 31, 1939.

The bill passed the House by a vote of 280-34 on May 4, 1934, and the Senate measure passed the upper house by a comparable majority, 62-13, on May 12, 1934. Before the bills went to conference for the ironing out of differences, President Roosevelt wrote to Senator Fletcher and Representative Rayburn urging that "the requirement of what is known as margin be made so high that speculation . . . will of necessity be drastically curtailed." It was apparent that the President favored

---

[8] The Senate Committee Report contained no dissenting or minority opinion. There was a minority report to the House signed by one man, Representative Merritt of Connecticut.

the House bill, but the Conference Committee compromised, adopting the House's standard for margin requirements and the Senate's provision for a separate and independent administrative commission. The Conference Report passed Congress on June 1, 1934, and the Securities Exchange Act, after four months of concentrated work, became law on June 6.

The Securities Exchange Act of 1934

The Act, as finally passed, closely conformed to the revised Fletcher-Rayburn bill. Its provisions on security credit, which remain in effect today, are contained in Sections 7 and 8 of the Act.[9] The salient provisions of these sections were as follows:

1. The Federal Reserve Board was given authority over initial extension and subsequent maintenance of credit on securities other than exempted securities.

2. Initial loan values were set at 55 per cent of the current market price or 100 per cent of the lowest market price during the preceding 36 calendar months or since July 1, 1933, whichever period was the shorter. But in no case was the loan value to exceed 75 per cent of the current market price.

3. Exchange members, and brokers and dealers transacting a security business through such members, could lend only on securities registered on a national securities exchange or exempted securities.

4. The Federal Reserve Board was given the power to regulate the carrying of undermargined accounts, the withdrawal of funds or securities, substitution or additional purchases of securities, the transfer of accounts from one lender to another, and margin requirements for short sales and arbitrage transactions.

5. Margin regulations were not to apply to existing loans until July 1, 1937.

6. The Act denied authority to the Federal Reserve to prohibit the following types of loans by others than members of national securities exchanges and brokers/dealers doing business through them: (a) loans made outside the ordinary course of business,

---

[9] Sections 7 and 8 are reproduced in full in Appendix I.

(b) loans on exempted securities, which included Federal, state and municipal issues and others given such status by the Securities and Exchange Commission, (c) loans to dealers to aid in financing the distribution of securities outside a national securities exchange, (d) bank loans on other than equity securities (e) and such other loans as the Board might exempt.

Under the Act, the Federal Reserve Board was given authority, with the exceptions noted above, to regulate security loans by others than exchange members and brokers and dealers, only when such loans are for the purpose of purchasing or carrying listed issues. Brokers and dealers were permitted to borrow on non-exempted securities only from member banks of the Federal Reserve System, non-member banks that agreed to comply with the Act, other members, brokers or dealers, or in emergency situations.

In many cases, the initial margin requirements set in the Act proved to be substantially lower than the maintenance margin requirements set by the New York Stock Exchange. These margin requirements were not designed to discourage trading when prices were low. They were designed rather to discourage "excessive speculation." Thus, smaller margins were required on less volatile stocks than on those that fluctuated widely. In particular, the initial margin requirements specified in the law were drawn with the hope that they would discourage pyramiding. Most stocks would have to rise sharply above their 3-year low prices before the holder could increase his borrowing.

While only initial margin requirements were suggested in the statute, the Federal Reserve Board was given specific authority over the "maintenance of credit" on securities as well.

SUMMARY OF THE ACT'S LEGISLATIVE HISTORY

The legislative history of the margin provisions of the Securities Exchange Act of 1934 indicates that sober counsels prevailed in Congress over the views of those who sought either to prohibit altogether the use of credit in purchasing or carrying securities or to impose regulations so complex or so drastic as to be very difficult or impossible to administer.

That margin regulation is designed primarily to regulate the use of credit rather than stock market activity or prices was stated in the law. Section 7 gives the Federal Reserve Board authority to regulate the extension of security credit "for the purpose of preventing the excessive use of credit for the purchase or carrying of securities." Moreover, it was only after extended Congressional debate that the administration of the margin provisions was assigned to the Federal Reserve Board, rather than to the Securities and Exchange Commission. The language of the statute and this assignment indicated that margin control, as adopted, was not designed primarily or specifically to protect the trader, small or large, from loss or to regulate the volume of speculation.

Rather, control of margins was aimed principally at the broader and more attainable objective of contributing to economic stability by giving the Federal Reserve Board authority to apply selective control to specified forms of security credit, with a view to making quantitative credit control more effective. Only in the sense that it prevents increases or decreases in security loans that are so large as to give rise to wide price changes does margin regulation also contribute to the stability of the stock market.

The wide discretion given the Federal Reserve Board in Sections 7 and 8 of the Securities Exchange Act of 1934 made the regulations adopted by the Board under the statute of primary importance. These regulations are considered in the next chapter.

Chapter 9

EVOLUTION OF SECURITY CREDIT
REGULATION UNDER THE ACT

Drafting the First Regulation

The provisions of the Securities Exchange Act of 1934 relating to margin regulation were to become effective October 1, 1934, less than four months after the enactment of the law. The Federal Reserve Board was required by the statute to prescribe rules and regulations applicable to security credit before this effective date.

No time was lost, therefore, in embarking on the task of drafting a basic regulation covering margin requirements. Staff members began to work at this job the day the Act became law. At the same time, the Board sought to ascertain how existing margin accounts would be affected by the standard for initial extensions of credit set forth in the law to guide the Federal Reserve Board. This was 55 per cent of the current market price or 100 per cent of the lowest price since July 1, 1933, but not more than 75 per cent of the current market price.

In July, the New York, Chicago [1] and San Francisco [1] Stock Exchanges were requested to obtain reports from their members on the status of customer margin accounts. Reports were received on more than 200,000 accounts representing over two-thirds of customer borrowing. These showed that the value of securities in all accounts was nearly twice as large as the amounts borrowed. Only 12,500 of the 200,000 accounts had debit balances in excess of 75% of the collateral, the maximum loan value possible under the statute. The survey indicated that the great

---

[1] Now parts of the Midwest and Pacific Coast Stock Exchanges respectively.

majority of accounts would be over-margined in relation to the statutory requirements, so that there would be no material curtailment of the ability to make new purchases.

In August, 1934, two months after enactment of the law, a first draft of the proposed Regulation T was prepared by the staff of the Federal Reserve Board. This and succeeding drafts were submitted to margin clerks of brokerage houses in the major cities for their criticisms.

The Federal Reserve Board issued the original Regulation T, its first security credit regulation, to be effective October 1, 1934. This regulation applied to credit extensions by brokers and dealers. Security loans by banks were not made subject to regulation until May 1, 1936, when Regulation U became effective.

Regulation T Principles

The basic principles that guided the Federal Reserve Board in drafting Regulation T were later described by Carl E. Parry, who became the director of the Board's Division of Security Loans, as follows: [2]

1. Simplicity.

2. A uniform margin requirement for all classes of transactions, rather than separate requirements for "particular transactions or classes of transactions."

3. A text in the language of brokers and margin clerks, not of bankers or lawyers.

4. The precise and unmistakable terminology appropriate for a statute that provides criminal penalties for violations.

5. "Accounts" considered as a relationship between customer and broker, and not in the bookkeeping sense of a record.

6. Consideration of the financial relations between customer and broker as a single relationship.

7. Appraisal of each transaction by its effect on the relation

---

[2] "Some Principles Underlying Regulation T," an unpublished address by Carl E. Parry before the Senior Margin Clerks Section of the Association of Stock Exchange Firms on December 15, 1938, available in the Federal Reserve Library, Washington, D.C.

between "the adjusted debit balance of the account and the maximum loan value of the securities in the account."

Original Provisions of Regulation T

Regulation T, as first issued, laid down Federal Reserve regulatory policy as regards three basic aspects of security loan regulation. These were:

1. The limitation of regulation to initial margin requirements, without reference to maintenance of margins after purchases.

2. Rules for substitutions and withdrawals in accounts which had become undermargined or "restricted" because a decline in security prices had reduced the customer's margin below the initial requirements of Regulation T.

3. Definition of non-purpose security loans which were not made subject to margin requirements.

Each of these aspects of security credit regulation is discussed more fully below.

Regulation T, as originally issued, adopted the standard for initial margin requirements contained in the statute, which evidently reflected the intent of Congress. This was a minimum margin of 45% of the current market price,[3] or as low as 25% under the alternative provision that the initial extension of credit could be up to 100% of the lowest market price of the security after July 1, 1933, but not more than 75% of the current market price. The upper limit in the margin formula was raised to 55% on February 1, 1936, and a flat 55% minimum margin requirement replaced the statutory formula with its alternative bases for minimum margins on April 1, 1936.

Regulation T was amended a number of times with respect to provisions other than the margin requirements themselves between 1934 and 1937. On December 3, 1937, the Board of Gov-

---

[3] Regulation T specifies the "maximum loan value," which is the limit to which credit can be extended by the broker to his customer on the market price of registered, non-exempt securities purchased. A "margin requirement," the term in general use, is the minimum equity that the customer must put up on securities. Maximum loan value regards the transaction from the lender's viewpoint; margin requirement from that of the borrower.

ernors of the Federal Reserve System announced a general revision of the Regulation, effective January 1, 1938, to "clarify and
simplify" its contents. This was the last general revision of Regulation T, although particular provisions have been amended from
time to time.

Regulation U

The Securities Exchange Act directed the Federal Reserve
Board to prescribe rules and regulations also for security loans
by others than exchange members and brokers and dealers transacting a business in securities through such members. Between
1934 and 1936, Regulation T was the only one applicable to
security loans. On March 25, 1936, the Board issued Regulation
U, effective May 1, 1936, applicable to all banks in the United
States.

Explaining its decision to issue Regulation U the Board said: [4]

> The Securities Exchange Act of 1934 required the Board to
> issue regulations with respect to loans on registered securities
> by brokers and dealers in securities. In order to prevent circum-
> vention of such regulations, the act also authorized the Board
> to issue regulations relating to loans made by banks and others
> for purchasing or carrying registered securities. For a year after
> October 1, 1934, the effective date of Regulation T, relating
> to loans by brokers and dealers, bank loans on securities to
> others than brokers and dealers had declined. In the autumn of
> 1935, however, the decline had ceased. Since liquidation of
> old security loans continued, it appeared that banks had been
> making new loans on securities. Margin requirements on loans
> by brokers increased during the period, largely as a result of
> the automatic operation of the statutory margin formula pre-
> scribed in Regulation T and partly because of the increase in
> margin requirements made by the Board effective February 1,
> 1936. As a result of these increases there was a growing differ-
> ential between the amount that could be borrowed on a given
> security from a broker and from a bank.
>
> In order to place borrowing for speculative purposes, whether
> from brokers or from banks, on as nearly an equal basis as the
> law and the differences in the nature of the enterprises would
> permit, and in order to place the Board of Governors in a bet-
> ter position to control a speculative expansion, the Board
> adopted Regulation U.

---

[4] Board of Governors, Federal Reserve System, *Annual Report*, 1936, p. 32.

The decision to issue Regulation U applicable to bank loans for purchasing and carrying registered securities was a major influence in the substitution of a flat 55% margin requirement for the statutory formula. The statutory formula was being abandoned, the Board explained, for three reasons:

1. Stock prices had advanced so far that a loan equal to 100% of the lowest price of the preceding 36 months had ceased to act as an anti-pyramiding device.

2. The formula was considered "unnecessarily onerous for banks, since few banks have a large volume of security loans or familiarity with market quotations."

3. A single figure expressed as a percentage of current market value is simple and easily understood.

The Federal Reserve Board was authorized by the statute to exempt from margin regulation specified classes of security loans made by others than brokers and dealers. Regulation U provided such exemption for a number of classes of loans, in addition to those specifically mentioned in the statute, such as loans to finance securities carried for customers by brokers and dealers subject to Regulation T, loans to finance transactions of registered odd-lot dealers, and loans to banks or foreign banking institutions.

Initial vs. Maintenance Margins

When the New York Stock Exchange established a minimum customer margin requirement for its member firms of 30% of the *debit balance* in 1933, this requirement applied not only at the time of purchase but at all times so long as the account was maintained. Whenever the customer's margin, as computed on the basis of current security quotations, would fall below the minimum set by the exchange, now 25% of the *market value*, the customer would have to put up additional margin or sell sufficient securities in the account to restore the margin at least to the minimum required level.[5]

The Federal Reserve Board, in drafting Regulation T, decided

---

[5] Minimum maintenance margins of 25% are now required also by the American and Pacific Coast Stock Exchanges, among others.

to impose only initial margin requirements, and to leave entirely to the lenders' discretion the maintainence of margins in the event of declines in prices of securities in a margin account.

The reasons why the Federal Reserve Board limited itself to initial margin requirements were outlined by Carl E. Parry as follows: [6]

1. "For the Board to require margins to be 'kept good,' and to require liquidations for this purpose if the customer defaults, might at times of market weakness bring about so much selling as to cause or accentuate a collapse in prices and by thus promoting instability defeat one of the primary long-term purposes of the regulation."

2. "No such rule is needed to further the controlling purpose of the regulation—to prevent unwarranted growth of speculation by preventing unwarranted growth of credit for speculative purposes. If a customer's original margin has been impaired by a movement of the market against him, that customer may indeed be still using every bit as much credit as he took out in the first place, but the important thing for the Federal Reserve Board is that the customer is not using any more credit than he took out in the first place and so is not currently contributing to the growth of credit."

Regulation T now specifically provides that credit initially extended without violation of the regulation may be maintained regardless of:

1. Reductions in equity due to declines in market price.
2. Securities ceasing to be registered or exempt.
3. Changes in initial margin requirements.

Substitutions and Withdrawals

To prevent circumvention of margin regulations, Regulations T and U have from the start limited transactions in restricted accounts. An account becomes "restricted" when its adjusted

---

[6] Unpublished address of Dr. Carl E. Parry, cited in footnote 2 above.

debit balance [7] exceeds the maximum loan value of the securities held under the current margin requirements.

Under Regulation T, a customer whose account is restricted may not effect a transaction which, in combination with any other transaction on the same day, would result in an increase in the adjusted debit balance or a withdrawal of cash or securities. From 1934 to December 31, 1937, substitutions of securities by sales and purchases, if completed within two business days, were considered a single transaction and so not subject to this prohibition. Since January 1, 1938, purchases and sales must be completed on the same day to be considered a single transaction.

The original Regulation T provided that a customer selling a security in a restricted account could not withdraw cash from the account so long as the debit balance continued to exceed the maximum loan value of the account. This resulted in so many complaints that, in the general revision of the regulation effective January 1, 1938, the customer, following sale of a security, was permitted to withdraw cash up to an amount equal to the initial margin required at the time. Since the then prevailing margin requirement was 40%, the customer could withdraw cash equal to 40% of the proceeds of the sale of securities in restricted accounts. Customers could also withdraw securities from restricted accounts by putting up cash equal to the maximum loan value of the securities being withdrawn to reduce the debit balance.

This withdrawal privilege automatically became more liberal when margin requirements were increased. With a 75% margin requirement, for example, much the larger part of the proceeds of sale of a security could theoretically be withdrawn from an account, so far as Regulation T was concerned, no matter how deficient the margin in the account might be. Hence, Regulations T and U were amended on July 5, 1945, when the margin requirement was lifted to 75% for the first time, to provide that proceeds from the sale of securities were to be retained in accounts and used to reduce the debit balances so long as they remained re-

---

[7] The "adjusted debit balance" as defined in Regulation T includes the current market value of securities sold short in the account and other specified items that could make it differ from the net debit balance of the account.

stricted.[8] This rule, which came to be known as the "incidental squeeze" because it prevented the purchase of another security following security sales in a restricted account, together with the higher level of margin requirements, contributed to a sharp contraction in the volume of security credit outstanding during 1946.

When margin requirements were later reduced, however, the strict withdrawal rules were relaxed, effective April 1, 1948.[9] Customers were permitted to make substitutions of securities on the same day in restricted accounts where no increase in total holdings or total credit resulted. This provision was not found satisfactory either, and on April 19, 1948 the "incidental squeeze" was completely eliminated and the liberal withdrawal rules prevailing before July 5, 1945 were reinstated. As before 1945, customers could withdraw securities by reducing the debit balance in an amount up to the withdrawn securities' maximum loan value. They could also withdraw cash in an amount equal to the current margin requirement for the securities sold in the account.

New Approach—1959

A new approach to the regulation of substitutions and withdrawals in restricted accounts was adopted by amendments to Regulation T and U that became effective June 15, 1959, when 90% margin requirements were in effect. Withdrawal of securities or cash from a restricted account was permitted by these amendments if cash, registered or exempted securities were deposited in the account in an amount at least equal to the specified "retention requirement." This requirement was fixed on June 15, 1959 at 50% of the current market value of securities sold or withdrawn. Thus, if securities sold in a restricted account brought $10,000, it became necessary to apply $5,000 to reduce the debit balance. The remaining $5,000 could then be withdrawn, even though the account would remain restricted, because the debit balance continued to exceed the maximum loan value under prevailing margin requirements.

---

[8] *Federal Reserve Bulletin*, August, 1945.
[9] *Federal Reserve Bulletin*, March, 1948.

Limitations of withdrawals from restricted accounts, it is evident, have been utilized to make high margin requirements more effective as a means of reducing the volume of security credit outstanding.

Non-purpose Loans

Security loans which were not for the purpose of buying or carrying securities (so-called "non-purpose loans") were not made subject to the margin regulations under the Securities Exchange Act. Manifestly, this immediately presented a perplexing administrative problem. How could non-purpose loans be distinguished from purpose loans?

According to Regulation T:

> Every extension of credit on a registered security shall be deemed . . . for the purpose of purchasing or carrying securities unless the customer shall file with the creditor a written declaration signed by the customer which shall state . . . that such credit is not for the purpose of purchasing or carrying securities.

Regulation U adopted a much less rigid procedure for non-purpose loans by banks. In determining whether a security loan was for a purpose other than to purchase or carry securities, a bank under the original Regulation U "could rely upon a statement signed by an officer of the bank or by the borrower with respect thereto, accepted by the bank in good faith." The difficulty of defining a non-purpose loan was thus further complicated by the need for defining "in good faith."

The Federal Reserve authorities were not satisfied with this procedure for identifying non-purpose loans. Early in 1947, the Board, trying to tighten up administration of Regulation U, exhorted bankers not to accept a signed statement at face value, but "to be alert to the circumstances surrounding the loan." [10] At a later date, the Board again attempted to clarify the concepts surrounding non-purpose loans. "Good faith," it said, "requires among other things, reasonable diligence to learn the truth." [11]

---

[10] *Federal Reserve Bulletin*, January, 1947.
[11] *Federal Reserve Bulletin*, September, 1953.

But the situation was still considered far from satisfactory. Consequently, in May, 1959, another attempt was made to come to grips with this elusive aspect of security credit regulation. Effective June 15, 1959, an amendment to Regulation U laid down the principle that, in determining that a security loan is not for the purpose of purchasing or carrying securities, a bank would need a statement signed by both the borrower and an officer. If the statement specified only what was not the purpose of the loan, it would have to be accompanied by a memorandum from the lending officer describing the purpose of the loan. All statements would, of course, have to be in good faith, but the new amendment added, "the officer must be alert to the circumstances surrounding the loan and the borrower and must have no information which would put a prudent man upon inquiry and if investigated with reasonable diligence would lead to the discovery of the falsity of the statement."

Credit on Securities Purchased with Rights

To avoid hampering the raising of new equity capital by industry, Regulations T and U have provided since 1946 that a lower margin requirement shall apply to securities acquired through the exercise of subscription rights. This was done under the statutory provision that authorized the Federal Reserve Board to prescribe lower margin requirements, "with respect to . . . specified securities or transactions, or classes of securities, or classes of transactions." Since 1949, special subscription accounts are authorized for securities purchased through the exercise of rights.

The margin requirement applicable to securities bought through subscription accounts was set at 50% in 1946, and was reduced to 25% in 1949. Both Regulation T and Regulation U were amended in 1949 to provide that additional securities could not be acquired in a special subscription account unless the full margin required in general accounts had been put up for issues held in a special subscription account more than nine months.

Administration of Margin Regulation

To administer margin regulation, the Federal Reserve Board set up a Division of Security Loans in November, 1934, shortly after Regulation T was issued. Carl E. Parry, who had taken an active part in drafting the original Regulation T, was appointed director.

The securities exchanges have cooperated actively in the administration of Regulation T. "The New York Stock Exchange," Dr. Parry said in the address quoted earlier in this chapter, "has undertaken ever since the regulation was first issued to perform certain collateral functions in connection with the regulation: to answer questions; to distribute official rulings; to consider and act upon requests from members for extensions of time within which to get from customers required margin or required cash payment. The Exchange also combats among the customers of members of the Exchange the practice of 'free riding' in margin accounts, and supplements Regulation T in other ways. All this work of the Exchange has been warmly supported by the Association of Stock Exchange Firms. The Association has also sponsored the organization of the Senior Margin Clerks' Section and encouraged the Section to work on problems arising out of Regulation T. . . . I do not see how anyone connected with the Federal Reserve can fail to appreciate the assistance in administering Regulation T that can be rendered and is being rendered by the Exchange, by the Association and by the Section."

The Division of Security Loans was dissolved with Dr. Parry's retirement in 1948, since familiarity with margin regulation made a separate division no longer necessary. Since then, questions relating to Regulation T have been referred to the securities exchange of which the brokerage firm is a member or the Federal Reserve Bank of the district in which the exchange is located. Questions relating to Regulation U are referred to the Federal Reserve Bank of the district in which the inquiry arises.

Yardsticks for Margin Regulation

The Securities Exchange Act of 1934 directed the Federal Reserve Board to regulate security credit "for the purpose of preventing the excessive use of credit for the purchase or carrying of securities."

What constitutes an "excessive use" of such credit?

Four yardsticks for judging what is excessive are possible.

The test, which conforms most closely to the language of the statute, is the volume of security credit outstanding. However, in periods such as 1945-47 when very high margin requirements were maintained even though the volume of security credit outstanding had been reduced, the emphasis in judging what is excessive was put on the potential rather than the actual amount of credit used to buy or carry securities.

A second yardstick is the volume of speculative activity in the security markets. Dr. Parry favored this test. Holding that margin regulation was designed to influence the volume of speculative activity, he said:

> From time to time in the United States speculation in securities has greatly overreached itself, as it did in 1929, in 1920, and on earlier occasions. And whenever speculation in securities had overreached itself, the consequences have been bad. . . . There are good grounds for the belief that one of the factors that caused speculation in securities to overreach itself at such times was trading in securities on margin. If there had not been so much speculation on margin, the total amount of speculation would have been smaller, and there would not have been so much speculation on margin if margin requirements had been higher.

A third test is the price behavior of the stock market. This may involve consideration of the rate of advance or decline in prices as well as the level of prices. In explaining its actions on margin requirements, the Board of Governors has often referred to the price action of the market. However, the emphasis has been placed on preventing increases or decreases in security credit that are so large as to contribute to wide fluctuations in stock prices, rather than on making the stability of stock prices, or a rise or fall in the price level, an end in itself. The reason for this

is that wide swings in the level of security prices in turn stimulate
expansion or contraction of the volume of security credit, because
of the pyramiding and anti-pyramiding effects discussed in
Chapter V.

Experience has shown that stock prices can undergo wide
fluctuations even when relatively small changes occur in the
volume of security credit outstanding.

A fourth yardstick has been general economic and credit conditions. When pursuing a given credit policy, whether one of
restriction or of expansion, the Board of Governors has been in-
clined to consider use of all the policy instruments available to it,
including margin changes. Some of the Board's actions in the
domain of margin regulation during the quarter century in which
such controls have been exercised can be best understood as
motivated by a desire to supplement its major instruments of
credit policy—open market operations, changes in legal reserve
requirements of member banks and discount rate changes—in
applying the over-all credit policy that the authorities were pursuing.

Appendix III, quoting explanations for margin changes given
in the annual reports of the Board of Governors of the Federal
Reserve System, indicates the extent to which each of these
basic objectives have motivated the actions taken by the Board
to regulate security credit under Section 7 of the Securities Exchange Act of 1934. The extent to which each yardstick has been
cited by the Board in ordering margin changes is shown in
Table VI. The effects of increases or decreases in margin requirements are considered in the following chapter.

SUMMARY

The Federal Reserve Board, after consultation with brokerage
houses throughout the country, embodied its basic principles of
margin regulation in its Regulation T, which governs extension
of credit by stock exchange members, brokers and dealers.

Regulation T, and Regulation U applicable to banks which
followed 19 months later, set initial but not maintenance margin
requirements. The right to withdraw cash following security

TABLE VI

YARDSTICKS CITED BY THE FEDERAL RESERVE BOARD OF GOVERNORS FOR CHANGES IN MARGIN REQUIREMENTS 1936-1958

Effective Date of Margin Changes	Change in Margin Requirement (percentage points)	Resulting Margin Requirement (percent)	Volume of Security Credit Outstanding	Volume of Speculative Activity	Price Behavior of Stock Market	General Economic and Credit Conditions
February 1, 1936 (increase)	+10	55	x	x	x	x
November 1, 1937 (reduction)	−15	40	x		x	x
February 5, 1945 (increase)	+10	50	x		x	x
July 5, 1945 (increase)	+25	75	x	x		x
January 21, 1946 (increase)	+25	100				x
February 1, 1947 (reduction)	−25	75	x		x	x
March 30, 1949 (reduction)	−25	50				x
January 17, 1951 (increase)	+25	75	x	x		x
February 20, 1953 (reduction)	−25	50	x			x
January 4, 1955 (increase)	+10	60	x	x		x
April 23, 1955 (increase)	+10	70	x	x		
January 16, 1958 (reduction)	−20	50	x	x	x	x
August 5, 1958 (increase)	+20	70	x		x	
October 16, 1958 (increase)	+20	90	x	x	x	x

sales in restricted accounts has been withdrawn or limited when high margin requirements have been in effect, as a supplementary measure to limit the volume of security credit.

The exemption granted non-purpose loans under Regulation U has been a troublesome administrative problem. More elaborate precautions to prevent evasion of the Regulation became effective June 15, 1959.

Recognition has been given in margin regulation to the importance of not hampering the raising of new capital by industry, through lower minimum margins for securities acquired through the exercise of subscription rights.

Four yardsticks for measuring what is "excessive use of credit for the purchase or carrying of securities" have been:

1. The volume of security credit in actual or potential use.
2. Speculative activity in the security markets.
3. Price behavior of the stock market.
4. General economic and credit conditions.

Chief emphasis has been placed, as the statute directs, on limiting the volume of security credit outstanding. Through such limitation on credit, the Board has sought to contribute to the stability of the level of stock prices and to lessening what it views as an excessive expansion of speculative activity.

Chapter 10

EFFECTS OF CHANGES IN MARGIN REGULATIONS

During the first quarter of a century of margin regulation by the Board of Governors of the Federal Reserve System between October 1, 1934 and October 1, 1959, minimum initial requirements were increased 9 times and reduced 5 times, apart from the period of variable margin requirements before April 1, 1936. The effect of these changes on the volume of security credit outstanding and on the functioning of the stock market can be studied by comparing their behavior before and after each change in initial minimum margins.

However, many factors other than changes in margin requirements affect the volume of security loans, stock exchange activity, the trend of stock prices and other developments in the security markets. Hence, any conclusions drawn from a comparison of what happened before and after a margin change must necessarily be tentative and merely indicative in character. They are based on the isolation of only one of the many influences that affect the security markets.

Record of Margin Requirement Changes

Regulation of margin requirements was inaugurated by the Board of Governors of the Federal Reserve System with Regulation T, effective October 1, 1934, the date set by Section 7 of the Securities Exchange Act of 1934. Between that date and February 1, 1936, margin requirements were set at the standard contained in the statute, which was between 25 and 45%, the amount being determined for each stock by the lowest price at which it had sold since July 1, 1933. On February 1, 1936, the requirement was changed to 55%, unless the lowest price at which a stock had sold since July 1, 1933 justified a lower margin down to a minimum of 25%.

Not until April 1, 1936 was the statutory formula abandoned and a uniform minimum margin requirement of 55% adopted. On May 1, 1936, Regulation U applied the same uniform minimum to loans by banks for purchasing and carrying securities.

Following the stock market's decline in 1937, the first change was made in the uniform minimum margin requirement. It was reduced to 40% on November 1 of that year. No change was made thereafter until February 5, 1945, a period of more than 7¼ years that included nearly the entire duration of World War II.

Between February 5, 1945 and October 16, 1958, margin requirements were changed 12 times. They were raised eight times and reduced four times during this period of more than 14 years, providing a record which makes possible an analysis of the consequences of margin changes under a variety of economic and financial conditions.

Since February 5, 1945, the shortest interval between changes in margin requirements by the Board of Governors was 71 days in 1958. The longest was three years, eight months and 22 days between April 23, 1955 and January 15, 1958. As many as three changes were made in a single year, 1958. No changes were ordered in only six of the 14 years following 1945. (See Chart XIV.)

Size of Margin Changes

The size of individual changes in margin requirements has varied greatly since a uniform minimum requirement was first established on April 1, 1936. Of the margin requirement increases, three were of 25 percentage points, two of 20 percentage points and three of 10 percentage points. Of margin decreases, three were of 25 percentage points, one of 20 percentage points and the initial reduction was of 15 percentage points.

As the following table shows, every one of the six changes between July 5, 1945 and January 5, 1955, a period of almost a decade, involved increases or decreases of 25 percentage points,

Chart XIV

FEDERAL RESERVE INITIAL MARGIN REQUIREMENTS

1934–1959 *

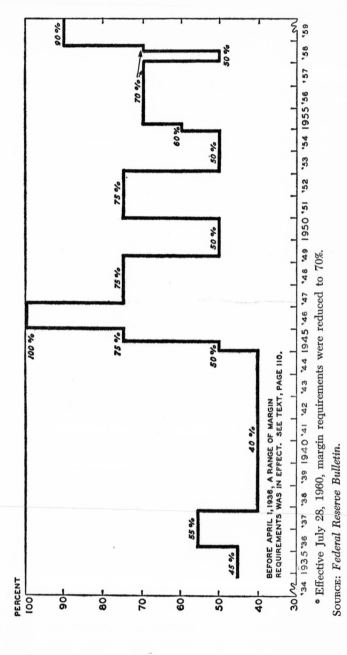

* Effective July 28, 1960, margin requirements were reduced to 70%.

Source: *Federal Reserve Bulletin.*

116

but both before and after this decade changes were of smaller magnitude:

TABLE VII

CHANGES IN MARGIN REQUIREMENTS
April 1, 1936 to October 16, 1958

Dates Effective	Margin Requirement (%)	Change from Previous Requirement (% Points)
April 1, 1936–November 10, 1937	55	
November 1, 1937–February 4, 1945	40	−15
February 5, 1945–July 4, 1945	50	+10
July 5, 1945–January 20, 1946	75	+25
January 21, 1946–January 31, 1947	100	+25
February 1, 1947–March 29, 1949	75	−25
March 30, 1949–January 16, 1951	50	−25
January 17, 1951–February 19, 1953	75	+25
February 20, 1953–January 4, 1955	50	−25
January 5, 1955–April 22, 1955	60	+10
April 23, 1955–January 15, 1958	70	+10
January 16, 1958–August 4, 1958	50	−20
August 5, 1958–October 15, 1958	70	+20
October 16, 1958	90	+20

Effect on the Volume of Security Credit

Changes in margin requirements affect in varying degree the volume of customer borrowing on registered stocks. This can be studied by measuring changes in the debit balances of customers of member firms of the New York Stock Exchange.

The table on page 118 shows the net change in such balances for the 6 months before and the 6 months after the month in which each margin increase or decrease became effective.

It will be noted that increases in customers' debit balances preceded a rise and decreases preceded a fall in margin requirements in each of these 13 cases except that of January 21, 1946, the one occasion when margin requirements were lifted to 100%. The increase from 75 to 100% on that date, despite a decline in customers' debit balances during the preceding 6 months, reflected a desire of the Federal Reserve authorities to utilize whatever restrictive measures remained available to them at a time

TABLE VIII

EFFECT OF CHANGES IN MARGIN REQUIREMENTS ON CUSTOMERS'
NET DEBIT BALANCES
November 1, 1937-October 16, 1958

Effective Date of Margin Change	Change in Customer Debit Balances in Preceding 6 Mos. (in millions)	Change in Margin Requirement (percentage points)	Change in Customer Debit Balances in Following 6 Mos. (in millions)
Increases			
February 5, 1945	+$130	+10	————
July 5, 1945	+ 161	+25	+$ 27.
January 21, 1946	— 64	+25	— 423
January 17, 1951	+ 102	+25	— 145
January 5, 1955	+ 570	+10	+ 222
April 23, 1955	+ 620	+10	+ 37
August 5, 1958	+ 557	+20	+ 257
October 16, 1958	+ 455	+20	+ 254
Decreases			
November 1, 1937	— 506	—15	— 274
February 1, 1947	— 212	—25	— 23
March 30, 1949	— 41	—25	+ 210
February 20, 1953	— 42	—25	+ 332
January 16, 1958	— 368	—20	+ 557

when pegging of the Government securities market by the Federal Reserve banks made the usual techniques of general or quantitative credit control inoperative. Moreover, the withdrawal restriction imposed on January 21, 1946 was followed by the largest decline in debit balances for any 6 months period since regulation of margins was inaugurated. This indicates the great effectiveness of limiting the withdrawal privilege in restricted accounts.

Changes in margin requirements have been followed in each case by a change in pace, if not in direction, of the trend of customer debit balances. The conclusions indicated by the behavior of customer debit balances following margin requirement changes are:

1. An increase in margin requirements during a period of ex-

pansion of customer debit balances slows up such expansion. This is shown by the amount of increase in debit balances for the 6 months before and after the margin increase in the 5 cases where the trend of debit balances continued upward after a higher margin requirement became effective:

Date of Margin Increase	Amount of Increase (percentage points)	Change in Customers' Net Debit Balances (in millions)	
		In 6 Months before Increase	In 6 Months after Increase
July 5, 1945	+25	+$161	+$ 27
January 5, 1955	+10	+ 570	+ 222
April 23, 1955	+10	+ 620	+ 37
August 5, 1958	+20	+ 557	+ 257
October 16, 1958	+20	+ 455	+ 254

2. In two instances, an increase in margin requirements either reversed or halted an upward trend in customers' debit balances during the preceding 6 months, and in a third a decline in debit balances was greatly accelerated when margin requirements were lifted to 100%.

3. Small increases in margin requirements were as effective as large ones in slowing down the rate of expansion of customer debit balances. The increase in margin requirements from 60% to 70% on April 23, 1955 was preceded by the largest 6-month increase of all those reported, $620 million. In the following 6 months, the increase was a negligible $37 million. The increase in margin requirements from 40 to 50% on February 5, 1945 came after a rise of $130 million in customer debit balances, but no change occurred in the 6 months following the increase.

4. Decreases in margin requirements were followed in each case by either an increase in customer debit balances or a marked slowing down of the preceding decrease.

Effect on Stock Prices

Changes in margin requirements have been one of the many factors that have both reflected and influenced the trend of stock prices, statistical evidence indicates.

The relation of margin requirement changes to stock prices is indicated in Table IX showing the percentage change in the Standard and Poor's composite index of 500 common stock prices for the 6 months before and the 6 months following each increase or decrease:

TABLE IX

MARGIN CHANGES AND THE TREND OF STOCK PRICES

Effective date of Margin Change	Change in Stock Price Average * in Preceding 6 Mos. (%)	Change in Margin Requirement (percentage points)	Change in Stock Price Index * in Following 6 Mos. (%)
Increases			
February 5, 1945	+ 7.7	+10	+ 6.7
July 5, 1945	+ 9.4	+25	+14.1
January 21, 1946	+17.4	+25	+ 1.3
January 17, 1951	+22.6	+25	+ 1.7
January 5, 1955	+16.7	+10	+14.8
April 23, 1955	+15.5	+10	+10.8
August 5, 1958	+11.6	+20	+12.9
October 16, 1958	+17.4	+20	+11.3
Decreases			
November 1, 1937	−26.6	−15	−12.3
February 1, 1947	−12.6	−25	+ 0.4
March 30, 1949	− 1.8	−25	+ 2.4
February 20, 1953	+ 2.7	−25	+ 5.2
January 16, 1958	−16.0	−20	+ 9.3

* Standard & Poor's Composite Index of 500 common stock prices.

Stock prices rose during the 6 months preceding each increase in margin requirements between 1937 and 1958. Prices declined in the 6 months preceding each reduction in margin requirements except one, that of February 20, 1953, and the rise in stock prices was quite small in that instance.

In the 6 months following each increase in margins, stock prices continued to advance. However, the amount of the rise was less than in the preceding 6 months in 6 of the 8 instances when margins were raised.

In the 6 months following each of the 5 reductions in margins, stock prices rose in 3 instances and declined in 2. In one of these 2 instances, the decline in the stock price index following the reduction in margin requirements was much smaller than that of the preceding 6 months.

In the light of the behavior of stock prices following changes in margin requirements, one may conclude that:

1. Increases in margin requirements in no case halted the rise in stock prices, but did slow down the rate of advance in 6 out of 8 instances.

2. Reductions in margin requirements were followed by an advance in stock prices or a slackening of the pace of a decline in every case.

Since the stock market's underlying trend was strongly upward over the whole of the first quarter of a century of margin regulation, and since a number of factors other than margin changes influence stock prices, the effects of past margin requirement changes may not be indicative of what may be experienced in the future.

Effect on Volume of Trading

A comparison of the number of shares traded on the New York Stock Exchange during the 6 months preceding and the 6 months following each change in margin requirements indicates that margin changes to date were a significant but not a predominant factor influencing activity on the Exchange. Since seasonal influences affect trading volume, it is desirable that adjustment be made for them in comparing turnover before and after each margin change.

The following table shows the trading volume in the 6 months preceding and the 6 months following each of the 13 changes in margin requirements from 1937 to 1958. The volume of trading figures have been adjusted seasonally beginning with the January 21, 1946 margin change, but seasonal adjustments are not available for earlier dates.[1]

---

[1] Seasonal adjustment factors for trading volume have been computed by the New York Stock Exchange.

TABLE X

Margin Changes and the Seasonally Adjusted Volume of Stock Trading

Effective Date of Margin Changes	Shares Traded on N.Y. Stock Exchange in Preceding 6 Mos. (millions)	Change in Margin Requirement (percentage points)	Shares Traded on N.Y. Stock Exchange in Following 6 Mos. (millions)
Increases			
February 5, 1945	144 *	+10	177 *
July 5, 1945	198 *	+25	179 *
January 21, 1946	210	+25	181
January 17, 1951	316	+25	232
January 5, 1955	341	+10	352
April 23, 1955	360	+10	327
August 5, 1958	322	+20	481
October 16, 1958	466	+20	404
Decreases			
November 1, 1937	163 *	−15	133 *
February 1, 1947	189	−25	141
March 30, 1949	142	−25	138
February 20, 1953	176	−25	184
January 16, 1958	303	−20	322

* Not seasonally adjusted.

During the period for which seasonally-adjusted data on Stock Exchange volume are available, increases in margin requirements were followed by a contraction of volume in 4 out of 6 cases. On the occasions when the increase in margin requirements was only 10 percentage points, the effect on volume was relatively small. Reductions in margin requirements were followed by an increase in the seasonally-adjusted volume in 2 out of 4 cases. Each of the 3 margin increases of 25 percentage points was followed by a material reduction in volume in the ensuing 6 months.

The period studied was one characterized by war, a post-war boom and a major inflation of the price level. Such conditions are highly favorable to equity investment. Whether the volume of trading would prove much more sensitive to sharp increases in margin requirements when economic conditions are less propitious to equity investment, only future experience can show.

Sharp Margin Increases and Acitivity in Low-Priced Stocks

A comparison for the ten weeks preceding and the ten weeks following increases of margin requirements to 70% or more shows that there may be some relationship between large margin increases and the proportion of low-priced shares among the 20 most active stocks.

Drastic increases in margin requirements have usually been accompanied by an increase in the proportion of low-priced issues among the 20 most active stocks. But small increases, even though margin requirements eventually reached a relatively high figure, have not had a similar effect. For example, when margin requirements were raised from 50 to 75 per cent in 1945, the number of low-priced issues [2] among the 20 most active stocks jumped from an average of 13.0 per week in the preceding ten weeks to an average of 14.7 in the ten weeks after the change. Similarly, when margins were raised from 50 to 75 per cent in 1949, the number of low-priced issues among the 20 most active stocks rose from an average of 12.0 per week to an average of 12.5. And in 1958, this pattern was repeated when margin requirements were raised from 50 to 70 per cent. In the ten weeks preceding August 5, 1958, an average of 5.9 out of the 20 most active issues were low-priced, while in the ten weeks after August 5 the average rose to 7.7.

In contrast, when requirements were raised only from 60 to 70 per cent in 1955, the 10-week average of low-priced stocks among the 20 most active issues dropped from 6.0 to 5.0.

There is thus some evidence that when margin requirements are raised sharply, public interest tends to increase in low-priced issues which involve a smaller cash outlay for purchases. The one exception occurred in 1946, when margin requirements were raised from 75 to 100 per cent and yet the number of low-priced stocks in the most active list dropped from an average of 13.8 to 13.3. (See Table XI.)

---

[2] Selling below $20.

TABLE XI

NUMBER OF STOCKS SELLING BELOW $20 AMONG 20 MOST ACTIVE STOCKS,
TEN WEEKS PRIOR TO AND TEN WEEKS AFTER INCREASES OF
MARGIN REQUIREMENTS TO 70 PER CENT OR MORE

Weeks Prior	Number of Stocks Under $20 Among 20 Most Active					
10th	13	15	13	8	5	4
9	13	12	13	8	4	9
8	14	13	12	3	3	8
7	10	16	12	5	9	18
6	12	15	11	6	10	11
5	13	12	12	6	9	9
4	15	12	12	8	7	6
3	15	13	12	8	2	9
2	13	15	11	5	5	7
1	12	15	12	3	5	5
Average	13.0	13.8	12.0	6.0	5.9	7.6
Effective Date	7/5/45	1/21/46	8/30/49	4/23/55	8/5/58	10/16/58
Margin Change	50 to 75%	75 to 100%	50 to 75%	60 to 70%	50 to 70%	70 to 90%
Weeks Following	Number of Stocks Under $20 Among 20 Most Active					
1st	15	18	12	4	4	6
2	16	15	12	6	9	8
3	14	16	12	9	8	9
4	16	13	14	4	8	7
5	16	13	13	4	11	8
6	15	12	13	5	9	8
7	14	11	10	3	6	6
8	13	11	13	4	9	10
9	13	11	13	6	8	6
10	15	13	13	5	5	6
Average	14.7	13.3	12.5	5.0	7.7	7.4

Effects of Changes in Withdrawal and Substitution Provisions

Changes in *initial* margin requirements have been the chief instrument of security credit regulation. Changes in withdrawal provisions can be an effective supplementary device, with changes in substitution provisions a possible final resort.

Margin requirements, applicable only to initial extensions of credit, limit the amount of new borrowing to purchase or carry securities. Restrictions on withdrawals and substitutions in margin accounts and bank security loans tend to reduce the amount of security credit outstanding. When limitations on withdrawals from restricted accounts were in effect between July 16, 1945 and April 1, 1948, a sharp decline in the volume of security credit outstanding occurred.

Changes in withdrawal restrictions can thus give the Board of Governors of the Federal Reserve System more complete control over the volume of security credit outstanding. This, in turn, lessens the size of increases in initial margins required to bring about a given reduction in the volume of security loans outstanding.

If security credit regulation is to rely more heavily on limitations on withdrawals of cash or securities from restricted accounts, therefore, data on the effects of such action upon the market are required. Such statistics can be derived from a periodic sample of margin accounts in stock exchange firms. By means of statistics from such a sample, the probable impact of changes in withdrawal and substitution and other regulations upon all margin accounts carried by New York Stock Exchange members can be appraised.

The Retention Requirement

Changes in Regulations T and U, effective June 15, 1959, limited withdrawals from restricted margin accounts and bank security loans by establishing a "retention requirement" of 50% of the proceeds of sale of a pledged security. The other 50% of the proceeds is to be used to reduce the debit balance in the restricted margin account or the amount due in the restricted bank loan.

Limitations on withdrawals of the proceeds of security sales from restricted margin accounts and loans necessarily reduce the ability of the owners to buy other securities, and so affect the liquidity the market provides to security owners. Sales of securities in restricted margin accounts and loans are thereby discouraged, since sellers who do not reinvest the proceeds on the same day will find the amount of securities they can carry reduced substantially. In practice, buying power in a restricted margin account is sometimes conserved by temporarily reinvesting the proceeds of sale of a stock on the same day in a short-term gilt-edge listed corporate obligation, which can later be sold to buy other stocks.

Revision of withdrawal and substitution rules could have effects fully comparable to those of margin changes on the purchasing power of margin accounts and the breadth of the market, so that changes in these rules would doubtless be made only after careful weighing of the consequences. Coordination of initial margin and retention requirement changes could well make relatively lower margin requirements more effective than was the case when initial margin requirements were relied upon exclusively to regulate the volume of security credit.

SUMMARY

The Board of Governors of the Federal Reserve System changed margin requirements by varying amounts and at varying intervals during the quarter century after October, 1934 when Regulation T first became effective. These changes permit study of the effects of margin increases and decreases.

Margin changes affected the trend of customer borrowing in each instance. Higher margin requirements have tended to restrain a rise in customers' net debit balances, while lowering of margin requirements has tended to slow up or reverse a decline in such balances. Small increases have generally been as effective as large ones in influencing the trend of customer borrowing.

Increases in margin requirements slowed but did not halt a rise in stock prices in most cases; reductions slackened or reversed a decline in stock prices in 4 out of 5 cases.

Evidence is less conclusive that margin changes have had a uniform effect upon the volume of trading on the exchanges. Up to the present time, at least, other influences have probably had a greater effect on volume.

Margin increases to 70% or more may increase trading interest in low-priced stocks, the statistical evidence indicates.

Margin regulation can be effected by changes in withdrawal and substitution provisions, as well as in initial margin requirements. In particular, an increase in the retention requirement applicable to the proceeds of sales of securities in restricted margin accounts can cause a substantial reduction in the volume of security loans outstanding, as well as in the purchasing power available to buy securities in margin accounts. Coordination of initial margin and retention requirements would provide the Federal Reserve authorities with a more sensitive instrument for regulating the volume of security credit outstanding, and so could lessen the need for very high margin requirements at times when economic conditions favor a large increase in security borrowing.

Chapter 11

UNREGULATED SOURCES OF SECURITY CREDIT

Avoidance of Regulations T and U

Regulation of security credit, to the extent that it is effective, at times must prevent many persons from borrowing as much as they would like for purchasing and carrying securities. This leads them to resort to types and sources of borrowing that are not subject to the restrictions imposed by Regulations T and U.

The problem of evasion of security credit regulation was recognized by Congress when it was drafting Section 7 of the Securities Exchange Act of 1934. It was evident from the start that regulation of brokerage house margin requirements by the Securities and Exchange Commission, as first proposed, would only serve to shift borrowing on securities into the banks whenever high margins were imposed. Hence Section 7(d) of the law, as enacted, authorized the Federal Reserve Board to regulate collateral loans for purchasing or carrying securities made by "any person," and to impose on such loans rules and regulations "similar to those imposed upon members, brokers, or dealers." Under this section, Regulation U was issued in 1936 to apply margin controls to commercial banks.

Until June 15, 1959, "persons" other than banks, brokers and dealers were not subject to regulation. Following amendment of Regulation U on that date, reports on security loans were required from "every person engaged in the business of extending credit who, in the ordinary course of business, extends credit" to purchase or carry registered stocks.

But a number of kinds and sources of borrowing to purchase or carry securities are not affected by the margin requirements set in Regulations T and U. The higher the margin requirements

128

imposed under these regulations, the greater the incentive to avoid them by those eager to use credit in purchasing and carrying securities.

America's experience with Prohibition demonstrated that a law which invites widespread evasion cannot fulfill the purpose for which it was enacted, and may have positive undesirable consequences.

There are three reasons why expansion of unregulated forms of security credit is of major significance in appraising the record of security credit regulation. These are:

1. Increased borrowing of this kind undermines the effectiveness of high margin requirements imposed under Regulations T and U when restriction of the volume of security credit is considered desirable by the Federal Reserve authorities.

2. The conditions for borrowing through unregulated channels may artificially stimulate the flow of funds into particular kinds of securities such as convertible bonds. This tends to distort the pattern of investing and the allocation of financial resources in the economy.

3. Loans on thin margins by lenders not subject to Federal Reserve regulations could have an adverse effect on security market stability where such lending attains substantial volume.

Unregulated Kinds of Security Credit

No complete catalogue of the types and sources of borrowing not subject to margin requirements under Regulations T and U can be compiled. Some are known, others only suspected. For the most part, statistics are not available to measure the volume of such borrowing.

When margin requirements are lifted high enough, many traders and investors seek to borrow in ways or from sources not subject to the provisions of Regulations T and U. Only the ingenuity of borrowers and lenders limits the character and variety of the expedients that are developed for borrowing on securities on more favorable margins than those specified in Regulations T and U.

Some unregulated sources of security credit have been little used to date. Others have been utilized to a substantial extent at times when margin requirements under Regulations T and U have been made quite high. But experience to date offers no assurance whatever that any or all of these methods of avoiding the regulations will not be used on a larger scale at some time in the future, when high margin requirements and expectations of advances in the security markets make this seem desirable to borrowers.

Major types and sources of security credit that are not subject to margin requirements laid down in the Federal Reserve regulations are:

1. Borrowing on exempted securities.
2. Borrowing from banks on bonds and unregistered stocks. Loans on unregistered stocks by banks are subject to Regulation U only if the proceeds are used to buy registered stocks.
3. "Non-purpose" loans that are used to buy or carry registered or unregistered securities.
4. Loans from sources other than brokers or banks, such as finance companies, used to purchase or carry registered or unregistered securities.
5. Loans from unregulated foreign lenders.
6. Repurchase agreements.

The potential extent and significance of each of these forms of credit not subject to the margin regulations will be discussed in this chapter.

Borrowing on Exempted Securities

The largest of the possible loopholes for expanding security credit without restraint from Regulations T and U is lending on U. S. Government, state and municipal securities. These classes of securities are expressly exempted from margin regulation as well as from other provisions of the Securities Exchange Act of 1934. Almost $250 billion of marketable exempted securities were outstanding at the end of 1959.

The New York Stock Exchange has set a minimum margin requirement of 5% of principal amount for U. S. Government securities and 15% for other exempted securities. The American,

Pacific Coast, and Philadelphia-Baltimore stock exchanges also have a 5% margin requirement for U. S. Government securities, and a requirement of 15% of cost or 25% of market, whichever is lower, for other exempted bonds.

The chief recent occasion when a considerable volume of U. S. Government securities was carried on margin was in the first half of 1958, when individuals sought to carry large amounts of these obligations on very thin margins through loans or by repurchase agreements. "Our study shows," Secretary of the Treasury Anderson and Chairman Martin of the Board of Governors of the Federal Reserve System reported in 1959, "that there was indeed a substantial volume of credit-financed participation in the June (1958) refunding—about $1.2 billion. . . . Speculation financed by credit created a particular problem in this instance because there were large blocks of holdings acquired by newcomers to the market who bought or made commitments to buy Government securities on very thin margin—or in many cases on no margin at all." [1]

The ability to buy and carry Government securities on extremely liberal credit terms attracted a far larger volume of purchases at the time than would have occurred otherwise.

A reversal of the Federal Reserve System's easy money policy produced large-scale liquidation, a break in prices and disorderly conditions in the Government security markets by the middle of 1958. Actually, purchases of U. S. Government securities financed with thinly margined loans and under repurchase agreements did not continue long enough and reach such proportions as to have lasting effects on the capital markets or the economy. Nevertheless, the episode did dramatize the possibility of a shift of margin trading to exempted securities at times when conditions are widely regarded as favorable for a rise in prices of such securities, as well as to center attention on unusually heavy speculation on thin margins as a specific threat to the stability of the market for Government securities.

Nevertheless, a survey in 1959 by the Treasury and Federal Reserve System showed most experts "felt it would be unde-

---

[1] *Federal Reserve Bulletin,* August, 1959, p. 865.

sirable to impose statutory margin requirements on purchases of Government securities, although there was general agreement that abuse of existing credit standards was undesirable and should be prevented. . . . It was claimed that such requirements would discourage participation in the market and would hinder the normal speculative activity that is necessary for the success of Treasury financings and for the efficient functioning of the market for Government securities." [2] These arguments were much the same as those advanced against the adoption of margin controls generally before enactment of the Securities Exchange Act of 1934.

However, the Comptroller of the Currency in April, 1960, directed national bank examiners to see that banks under their supervision require a margin of at least 5% on loans secured by Government obligations or on repurchase agreements covering Government securities. The primary purpose of this action was to protect the lending banks. "Fluctuations in the price of Government securities in certain instances," the letter to chief bank examiners said, "might raise questions as to the propriety and soundness of loans made by banks secured by and dependent on such securities without adequate margin."

The Comptroller added that "extension of credit without adequate margin for the purpose of carrying speculative positions in Government securities was a contributing factor to the disruptive fluctuation in Government securities prices during the late spring and summer of 1958." There was thus an intent also to safeguard the stability of the Government security market.

The Comptroller's letter provided for flexibility in the application of the 5% margin requirement for national bank loans on Government securities. A lower margin could be required for short-term issues, and the margin could be higher or lower according to "the circumstances of a particular credit." This flexibility reflected the desire of the Comptroller to minimize the adverse effect of minimum margins on the breadth of the market for U. S. Government obligations.

In May, 1960, the New York State Banking Department ruled

---

[2] *Treasury-Federal Reserve Study of the Government Securities Market, 1959, Part I,* (Washington: Government Printing Office, 1959), pp. 40-41.

that state-chartered banks must require a minimum of 5% margin on loans secured by U. S. Government obligations. The new requirement would particularly affect the big New York City banks, most of which are chartered by the state.

Proportion of Security Loans Secured by U. S. Governments

The proportion of loans secured by U. S. Government obligations to total loans to customers for purchasing and carrying securities has varied as shown on Chart XV since 1944. The World War II period and the 1958 episode apart, it is apparent that such loans have constituted a relatively small proportion of total security credit. However, in view of the huge size of the public debt, loans secured by U. S. Government obligations and credit extended through repurchase agreements covering such issues remain a major potential source of security credit expansion outside the controls provided by Regulations T and U. For example, on June 20, 1945, when a new Treasury offering was being distributed, $1.7 billion of $2.6 billion of reporting member banks' security loans to brokers and dealers, and $2.0 out of $2.4 billion of such loans to other borrowers, were secured by U. S. Government obligations.

It is doubtful that loans to individual investors secured by tax-exempt state and municipal bonds will ever assume significant proportions, since the interest paid on loans to purchase or carry such securities may not be deducted from taxable income.

Borrowing from Banks on Bonds and Unlisted Stocks

The intent of Congress, in drafting Section 7(d) of the Securities Exchange Act of 1934, was "to prevent the banks from being used for the purpose of circumventing the margin requirements prescribed for loans extended by brokers to their customers." [3] Obviously, such circumvention on a large scale would nullify the effectiveness of margin control.

Nevertheless, Regulation U has been far less restrictive in regulating bank security loans than Regulation T has been in

---

[3] Statement by the Secretary of the Federal Reserve Board, July 5, 1934.

Chart XV

PROPORTION OF LOANS ON GOVERNMENTS TO TOTAL SECURITY LOANS
1944–1959 *

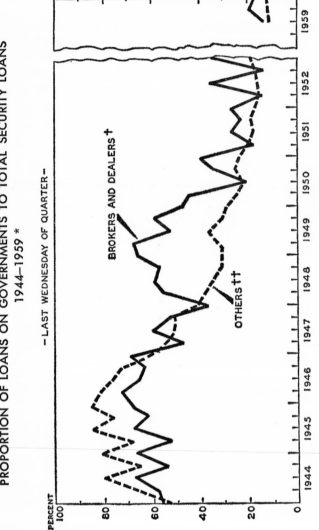

* Loans by weekly reporting Federal Reserve member banks. 1953-58 not available. † Loans to brokers and dealers secured by U. S. Government obligations as percent of total loans to brokers and dealers. †† Loans to others secured by U. S. Government obligations as percent of total loans to others.
SOURCE: New York Stock Exchange from data of Federal Reserve Board.

regulating the extension of credit by brokers. Banks can make a number of types of loans for purchasing and carrying securities that are not subject to margin control, whereas brokers would either require the minimum margin under Regulation T or be barred altogether from lending on such securities.

The following types of loans to purchase or carry securities are not subject to margin regulation when made by banks:

1. Loans secured by stocks for the purpose of purchasing either registered bonds or unregistered stocks and bonds. Regulation U applies only to loans "secured directly or indirectly by any stock for the purpose of purchasing or carrying any stock registered on a national securities exchange."

2. Loans secured by registered bonds for the purpose of purchasing or carrying any securities. Section 7(d) of the Securities Exchange Act of 1934 excludes loans made by banks on "non-equity securities" from margin control by the Board of Governors of the Federal Reserve System. As a result, Regulation U could be made applicable to convertible registered bonds, which come under the definition of an "equity security" because they are convertible into stock, but not to other bonds. Regulation U has not set margin requirements on loans secured by convertible registered bonds. Only when such bonds are converted and the stock received in exchange is substituted as collateral do the margin regulations apply to the loan.

3. Loans secured by unregistered securities when the proceeds are not used for the purpose of purchasing or carrying registered stocks. The Securities Exchange Act does not authorize the Board of Governors to regulate loans on unregistered security collateral for the purpose of purchasing either registered bonds or unregistered securities of any kind.

Estimates made by the New York Stock Exchange indicate that there were over $300 billion of corporate bonds and unregistered stocks outstanding on June 30, 1960 on which security loans by banks would not be subject to margin regulation. This presents a possible loophole for expansion of security credit that cannot be closed under existing law, and the Board of Governors could close it only if the Act were first amended.

Action Required to Bring Excepted Loans Under Regulation

To bring under the margin requirements set by Regulations T and U the several types of bank security loans that are not now subject to regulation, the following actions would have to be taken:

TYPE OF BANK SECURITY LOAN	ACTION REQUIRED TO BRING UNDER REGULATION
Bank loans on registered or unregistered bonds for the purpose of buying or carrying registered or unregistered securities	Amendment of the Securities Exchange Act of 1934.
Bank loans on registered stocks for the purpose of buying or carrying registered bonds	Change in Regulation U.
Bank loans on registered stocks for the purpose of buying or carrying unregistered securities	Amendment of the Securities Exchange Act of 1934.
Bank loans on convertible registered bonds	Change in Regulation U.
Bank loans on unregistered stocks to purchase unregistered securities	Amendment of the Securities Exchange Act of 1934.
Bank loans on unregistered stocks to purchase registered securities	Change in Regulation U.
Bank loans on U. S. Government and other exempt securities	Amendment of the Securities Exchange Act of 1934.

"Non-Purpose" Loans from Banks

Section 7 of the Securities Exchange Act authorizes margin regulation for loans "for the purpose of purchasing or carrying" securities. Loans secured by stocks and bonds for other purposes, so-called "non-purpose" loans, have not hitherto been subject to margin requirements. This is true whether the "non-purpose" loans are made by brokers or banks. The question of whether margin regulations can be applied to "non-purpose" loans has been the subject of differences of legal opinion.

In the relatively rare cases of "non-purpose" extensions of

credit by brokers as an accommodation to customers, Regulation T requires a written declaration signed by the customer stating the use to be made of the credit, as well as the statement that such credit is not for the purpose of purchasing, carrying or trading in securities. This requirement and the policy of many stock exchange firms have discouraged "non-purpose" borrowing by brokerage house customers.

In the case of "non-purpose" loans by banks, Regulation U until June 15, 1959 required only a statement that the loan was not for the purpose of purchasing or carrying registered stocks. This statement, accepted by the bank in good faith, could be signed by an officer of the bank or the borrower. Regulation U was amended on June 15, 1959 to provide that the statement of "non-purpose" must be signed by both the borrower and the lending officer. If the purpose of the loan is not stated, the lending officer must provide a memorandum or notation describing the loan's purpose.

The proportion of "non-purpose" loans that may be used to help finance the purchasing and carrying of securities is not subject even to very rough estimate. Difficulties of policing such lending have often been recognized. Chairman Martin of the Board of Governors of the Federal Reserve System, testifying before the Fulbright Committee in 1954, said:

> Our bank examiners are watching it all the time. . . . We feel that there definitely is some leakage.[4]

A statement issued by the Board of Governors of the Federal Reserve System in March, 1960 said:

> The Board is concerned with evasive extensions of bank credit for the purpose of carrying registered stocks and expects banks to be alert in detecting and preventing attempts to circumvent the basic purpose of this regulation.

Even if all "non-purpose" loans are incurred strictly for business or consumption purposes, calling of thinly-margined loans of this character because of a stock market decline could lead to forced liquidation that would undermine the stability of the

---

[4] *Stock Market Study*, Hearings before Committee on Banking and Currency, U. S. Senate, 1955, pp. 553, 594.

market and so could give rise to untimely credit contraction. The practical effects on the volume of bank credit outstanding and on the security markets could thus be very similar to those which result from making purpose loans on relatively thin margins, as occurred in the days before Federal margin regulation.

The Volume of "Non-Purpose" Loans

Loans on stock and bond collateral for purposes other than purchasing and carrying securities have not been included by banks in the reported totals of security loans since 1938. Such loans made for business purposes are included with commercial and industrial loans; those made for consumption purposes are included with "other" loans.

Fragmentary statistical data on "non-purpose" loans indicate, however, that such borrowing has increased far more than total bank loans during recent years of relatively tight money and high margin requirements.

A spot survey made in 1946 indicated that business loans by Federal Reserve member banks secured by stocks and bonds, including U. S. Government bonds, totaled $945 million. This survey was described in the Staff Report to the Fulbright Committee as follows:

> A survey of Federal Reserve member banks as of November 20, 1946, covering business loans only, found that loans amounting to $945 million, or about 7 per cent of the total of $13.2 billion of business loans outstanding, were secured by stocks and bonds. At the end of 1946, member bank loans outstanding reported for the purpose of purchasing or carrying securities were $3 billion. Thus there were $3.9 billion of member bank business and security loans with securities as collateral, and of this total three-quarters were used for the purpose of purchasing or carrying securities. With loans on United States Government securities excluded from the business loans on securities, the total reported "purpose" loans were more than four-fifths of the $3.5 billion total.[5]

Early in 1955, a spot survey of all loans secured by stocks and

---

[5] *Factors Affecting the Stock Market,* Staff Report to the Committee on Banking and Currency, United States Senate, Washington, D.C.: Government Printing Office (1955), p. 45.

bonds was made by the Federal Reserve banks at the request of Senator Fulbright. This survey

> found that loans secured by stocks and bonds represented nearly 15 per cent of total loans, including business loans as well as "other" loans. "Purpose" loans to brokers and dealers were about 7 per cent of total loans; "purpose" loans to others, 3 per cent; and "non-purpose" loans 5 per cent. If the same relationship held for the approximately 6,400 other member banks, the total amount of such "non-purpose" loans on securities collateral at all member banks was approximately $3 billion.[6]

The 1946 survey covered only business "non-purpose" loans, while the 1955 survey included all such loans. While the second survey was more comprehensive, "non-purpose" loans for other than business purposes were doubtless very small in 1946, when output of durable goods and home building were curtailed because the economy was still in process of reconversion from a war to a civilian basis. Moreover, purchases of durable goods could be financed readily in other ways.

On both dates, business loans doubtless accounted for the bulk of "non-purpose" collateral borrowing. A comparison of figures for the two dates indicates that "non-purpose" loans on security collateral not only tripled in volume from 1946 to 1955, but also that the increase was considerably greater than that of purpose loans. "Non-purpose" collateral loans of the member banks were about a fourth of their security collateral loans in 1946 and a third in 1955.

A further increase in "non-purpose" loans on securities by member banks since the 1955 survey is indicated by comparative data for member state banks and trust companies in the Second Federal Reserve District. Between the 1954 and 1958 examination dates, increases in "other loans secured by readily marketable securities" by these banks far and away exceeded the increase reported in security loans to brokers. All of the latter were purpose loans, whereas "other loans secured by readily marketable securities" include "non-purpose" loans. (See Table XII.)

---

[6] *Ibid.*, p. 46. However, a survey of the security pledged on business loans by member banks of the Federal Reserve System on October 5, 1955 showed that only $1.3 of the $30.8 billion of loans to business on that date listed bonds and stocks specifically. This may indicate that the estimate in the Staff Report was too large. See *Federal Reserve Bulletin* for September, 1959, pp. 1114-1129.

TABLE XII

LOANS BY MEMBER STATE BANKS AND TRUST COMPANIES
IN THE SECOND FEDERAL RESERVE DISTRICT
(in millions)

| | Examination Dates in | | % |
	1954	1958	Increase
Loans to brokers and dealers	$970.	$1,189.	23.
Other loans secured by readily marketable securities *	633.	2,583.	308.
Total loans (before valuation reserves)	12,245.	16,060.	31.
% security loans to total loans (average)	13.1	23.5	
Number of banks	168	164	

* Excluding loans secured by U. S. Government issues but including those secured by active over-the-counter stocks and listed and unlisted bonds.

Available data thus indicate that "non-purpose" loans on stock and bond collateral increased from 1954 to 1958, so that avoidance of margin regulation by the use of such loans may have become more prevalent in those years. The tightening up of the "non-purpose" loan procedure under Regulation U indicates that supervisory authorities believed this to be true. Nevertheless, the dollar volume of "non-purpose" loans actually being used to purchase or carry securities still had to be judged as moderate in 1958, since the aggregate of "non-purpose" loans was smaller than the volume of purpose loans (see pages 23-25).

"Non-purpose" loans on securities by banks, like loans on exempted issues, corporate bonds and unregistered securities, have constituted potential rather than actual channels for large-scale evasion of margin regulations. The amendments to Regulation U that became effective June 15, 1959 reflected the desire of the Federal Reserve authorities to lessen the possibility that "non-purpose" loans might be used for large-scale evasion of margin regulations during a period of high margin requirements and advancing stock prices. Other proposals to prevent evasion of Federal Reserve margin regulations have been advanced by supervisory officials, such as a requirement that "non-purpose" security loans shall contain provision for gradual repayment over a specified period of time.

Security Loans by Unregulated Lenders

While the Securities Exchange Act grants the Board of Governors authority to regulate collateral loans made by "any person" for the purpose of purchasing or carrying any non-exempt security registered on a "national securities exchange," the Board has not applied margin regulations to lenders other than brokers, dealers and banks.

Some factoring organizations of moderate size were soliciting stock market loans on a 20% margin basis in 1959, when 90% margins were required under Regulations T and U. Rates of interest were reliably reported to be 1½% per month or 18% a year on such credit.

An indeterminate amount of personal loans from banks and personal loan companies, policy loans from insurance companies, mortgage loans, borrowing from credit unions and loans from other sources is used for purchasing or carrying securities, but is not subject to regulation as such. The higher the margin requirements imposed by Regulations T and U, the greater the incentive to borrow from such sources not subject to Federal margin regulations.

The Board of Governors recognized the potential, if not the actual, importance of unregulated lenders on securities when it amended Regulation U on June 15, 1959 to provide that the Board may require reports not only from banks, but also from "every person engaged in the business of extending credit who, in the ordinary course of business, extends credit for the purpose of purchasing or carrying securities registered on a national securities exchange." The amended regulation specifically stated that such reports shall be made "as the Board of Governors of the Federal Reserve System may require to enable it to perform the functions conferred upon it by the Securities Exchange Act of 1934." This was followed by a requirement that previously unregulated lenders report on the types, purposes and collateral of the loans they make secured by listed issues, a move that could be a prelude to further regulatory steps.

Moreover, the exemption previously given loans not secured, directly or indirectly, by at least some stock was discontinued "as to loans made to companies engaged principally, or as one of the company's important activities, in making loans on an exempt basis to finance the purchase of registered stocks." This change in Regulation U resulted from known instances of finance companies that utilized unsecured lines of credit from banks to borrow funds for lending on stocks on thin margins at high rates of interest.

While there are no available statistics on the volume of security lending by lenders other than brokers and banks, the total of such credit could well be substantial at times when high margin requirements prevail. However, based on experience to date, lending on securities by such unregulated lenders has been more a potential than an actual threat to the effectiveness of margin regulation.

Loans from Foreign Lenders

Foreign banks have become a substantial source of security loans for American borrowers. Section 8 of the Securities Exchange Act makes it unlawful for brokers and dealers to borrow from non-member banks, unless the latter file an agreement with the Board of Governors to abide by margin regulations applicable to member banks. A special form of agreement has been prepared for a bank that "has an office or agency in the United States and its principal place of business outside the United States."

Loans on securities from foreign lenders have been negotiated for the most part by agencies of foreign banks in New York and by money brokers. An indication of the volume of such loans is given by statistics of call loans made by Canadian banks to brokers and dealers outside Canada, shown on the combined statement of Canadian chartered banks. At the end of May, 1960, such loans were reported at $980 million, a peak since they were first reported. Security loans by Canadian and Swiss bank agencies in the United States, by far the most important of such lenders, were reported to be secured for the most part by U. S. Government issues and convertible bonds.

An indeterminate amount of borrowing on securities from foreign sources is also arranged directly or through individual intermediaries. Publicity was given this type of lending during the battle for control of Fairbanks Morse & Co. in 1958 and proceedings of the Securities and Exchange Commission against Alexander Guterma, Matthew M. Fox and others in 1959 and 1960. Such lending tends to be limited to larger loans because of the negotiation problems involved. Interest rates on foreign bank loans on listed American stocks at a high ratio of market value were reported in financial circles to be 12% and more in 1959.

Loans Through Money Brokers

Money brokers, who arrange loans between borrower and lender for a fee, have long been active in the arrangement of security loans. Their role has been particularly important in arranging for bank loans on bonds, which are not subject to Regulation U, from institutions in areas where a surplus of loanable funds exists.

Because of the large volume of credit for buying or holding Government securities used in 1957 and 1958, the role of money brokers came under particular scrutiny at that time. The Treasury-Federal Reserve Study, referring to very large purchases of Treasury issues maturing in June, 1958 for exchange into new bonds then being offered, said:

> The activities of one Stock Exchange member specializing in money brokerage facilitated the financing of a substantial volume of the June rights. The operations were found to be in violation of Stock Exchange rules.[7]

Repurchase Agreements

A repurchase agreement arises out of the sale of a security under a contract in which the seller agrees to buy back the identical security on a specified date and at a specified price. The repurchase price will usually exceed the sale price by an amount equal to the rate of return to be paid the buyer, except where the buyer gets his return through collecting interest that becomes payable on the security.

---

[7] *Federal Reserve Bulletin*, August, 1959, p. 865.

The repurchase agreement permits a grant of credit of virtually 100 per cent of the value of a security to the seller, who agrees to buy back at a stated price. The "buyer" actually assumes no price risk so long as the seller honors his commitment to repurchase. Hence, where it can be used, it is a particularly effective means of obtaining credit to finance securities transactions outside the scope of margin requirements.

This device has thus far been used on any material scale only in the case of U. S. Government securities, which are exempt from Federal Reserve margin regulation although subject to a minimum margin requirement of the New York Stock Exchange.

Business corporations as well as banks have entered extensively into repurchase agreements for Government securities. While these agreements are usually arranged with dealers, in 1958 a number were entered into with individuals also. The Treasury-Federal Reserve Study of the Government Securities Market reported on the 1958 experience as follows: [8]

> In the speculative market build-up the use of the repurchase form of credit financing as a vehicle of nonprofessional and unsophisticated participants proved to be unsound. Use of this particular type of financing instrument, in effect, resulted in lenders' advancing credit to unknown borrowers of unknown credit standing or capacity.
>
> Even among known borrowers of professional standing, the use of the repurchase agreement device was stretched in terms of the types of the security which it covered. In the past, this instrument was employed in the dealer market mainly to finance securities of the shortest term. In its 1958 market usage, the instrument was extended in numerous instances to longer term securities where the maturity bore little or no relationship to the date of termination of the agreement.
>
> Where used in the mid-1958 period to finance holdings of longer term securities, the repurchase agreement technique in some cases provided a convenient means to circumvent owners' equity requirements that would have been applicable on loans, through margins required by lenders.

Explicit recognition was thus given for the first time to the "repurchase form of credit financing" as a device for circumventing security loan standards.

---

[8] *Federal Reserve Bulletin*, August, 1959, pp. 867-8.

The repurchase agreement could be used for financing the purchase and holding of securities other than U. S. Government obligations where the credit of the person obligated to repurchase the security at the end of the specified period is strong. Hence, it is another potential method for financing security purchases outside of Regulations T and U.[9]

SUMMARY

A number of types and sources of security credit are not subject to Regulations T and U of the Board of Governors of the Federal Reserve System. The more important of these are: (a) loans on exempted securities, (b) loans by banks on bonds, (c) bank loans on unregistered stocks except where the proceeds are used to buy registered stocks, (d) "non-purpose" loans used to buy or carry securities, (e) loans from sources other than brokers or banks, (f) loans from foreign lenders and (g) repurchase agreements.

There is evidence that each of these unregulated sources of security credit has been used to a degree, especially at times when high margin requirements were in effect under the regulations. This has been particularly true of "non-purpose" loans by banks and loans from sources other than brokers or banks. Each of these types and sources of credit could prove a major channel of credit expansion and avoidance of Regulations T and U in a future period of protracted high margin requirements and rising security prices. Instances of loans on common stocks at a very high percentage of market value, and bearing high rates of interest, were brought to light in SEC proceedings in 1959-1960.

Moreover, by encouraging trading and investment in exempt bonds, convertible bonds and unlisted issues to escape high margin requirements, these unregulated sources of credit can distort the distribution of funds among the several classes of securities. A dramatic example of this tendency was the wave of public buying of U. S. Government securities on very thin margins and under repurchase agreements during the first half of 1958.

---

[9] However, no broker or dealer subject to Regulation T may arrange such repurchase agreements on non-exempt securities, without violating Section 7(a) of Regulation T.

Chapter 12

SUMMARY OF FINDINGS
AND MAJOR CONCLUSIONS

Facts and
Analysis on

Historic Role

Several features of the American economy explain why security credit has played a vital role in the economic development of the United States almost from the nation's inception.

On the one hand, the rapid growth of the American economy has made necessary the issuance of stocks and bonds in huge amounts to raise needed capital. Security loans have played an indispensable part in financing the distribution of these securities, in broadening the market for them, and in enabling security owners to borrow money on their holdings when the need arose.

On the other hand, the unit banking system compelled the larger banks in the financial centers to maintain a high degree of liquidity to be ready for withdrawals of funds by their correspondents. Call loans on securities were the favored liquidity medium of banks in financial centers over the larger part of the nation's financial history.

While the economic benefits of security credit were widely recognized, this form of lending attracted critical attention during the several "money panics" that occurred before 1913. These episodes resulted when strains in the economy led to wholesale withdrawals of balances from financial centers. The consequent shortage of loanable funds, which caused call money rates to be bid up to fantastic levels at the culmination of these panics, led to forced liquidation of securities and so contributed to acute weakness in the security markets.   *Pages 1 to 6*

Under the Federal Reserve System

The pooling of bank reserves in the Federal Reserve System has made money panics a thing of the past. Hence, while security loans have become far less important to banks as a source of liquidity, their usefulness to borrowers has been enhanced by elimination of the danger of a concerted calling of loans and extreme increases in interest rates.

The use of security credit has expanded under the Federal Reserve System, contrary to some of the prophecies made when the Federal Reserve Act was enacted. Its advantages to borrowers and lenders, as well as to the economy, explain its growth.

However, the abnormal bulge in the volume of security loans in the late 1920's, and the very rapid deflation of such credit that followed, demonstrated that general credit control by the Federal Reserve System could not cope with an episode of this kind. Wide fluctuations in the volume of security loans undermined the effectiveness of quantitative credit control for a time. The desire to prevent a repetition of that experience led to the inauguration of selective regulation of security credit under the Securities Exchange Act of 1934.   *Pages 6 to 10*

Uses of Security Credit

Few forms of credit, if any, have as many varied uses as security loans. These include:

1. Financing the origination and distribution of security issues and the carrying of inventories by security dealers. In view of the very large amounts of credit required by security underwriters and dealers relative to their own capital, there is no other method available to finance this vital segment of a free enterprise economy.

2. Borrowing by investors and speculators for a wide variety of reasons, among which the quest for capital appreciation is but one. Anticipatory investment of future income, financing of pre-emptive subscriptions offered stockholders, profiting from a differential between investment yields and borrowing costs, and the exercise of restricted stock options by corporate officials or employees are other reasons for borrowing to purchase or carry securities.

3. Loans for business or consumption purposes which are made possible or facilitated by the pledge of securities as collateral. In many cases, such loans could not be arranged at all without collateral to protect the lender. In other instances, the lender would advance a much smaller sum without collateral. Almost invariably, the rate of interest charged would be a good deal higher without the protection given the lender by the pledge of securities as collateral.

4. Providing an attractive outlet for funds to lenders because of their high quality and liquidity. For banks, however, short-term U. S. Government obligations have replaced security loans as a prime liquidity medium since the available supply of such issues has been enormously swelled with the great increase in the public debt. *Pages 12 to 30*

Economic Effects

The contribution of security credit to economic growth has been far greater than the average volume of such loans would indicate.

An essential prerequisite for economic growth is capital formation. The security markets play a key role in capital formation. They enable business enterprises and governments to raise funds for capital investment by new security flotations. In addition, because corporate stockholders can readily sell their shares in the market if they need cash, they are willing to have a large part of current profits reinvested to finance expansion, rather than paid out to them as earned.

Security credit, in turn, is essential to the functioning of the security markets. "Wholesale" security credit finances both new flotations and the carrying of inventories by those who make markets in outstanding issues. "Retail" security credit, by expanding the number of those who can buy or carry securities, broadens the market for both new and old issues.

In addition to fostering growth of the economy, security credit also enhances its liquidity. Holders do not have to sell their securities should the need arise to raise cash, since funds can be obtained also by pledging the securities as collateral for loans. The increase in liquidity thus obtained contributes to the stability of the economy, as well as fostering its growth.   *Pages 35 to 38*

The security markets do not absorb credit. They provide basically a conduit through which funds are transferred from buyers to sellers of securities. Hence, an increase in security loans causes a transfer of the funds borrowed to the sellers of securities. If the sellers are corporate issuers of new securities, the expansion of security credit results in business capital formation. If the sellers are investors who dispose of outstanding securities, the proceeds of the security loans are used for productive or consumptive purposes, according to what the sellers do with the money.

In other words, an increase of security credit results in an expansion of funds available for business or consumption spending just as would an increase in other types of credit. Conversely, a decline in security credit reduces the volume of funds available for business or consumer spending. The effect on the economy as a whole and on the price level tends to be the same as the expansion or contraction of any other form of credit.

A sharp expansion or contraction of security loans, as of other types of credit, does contribute to economic instability. This was made apparent by the experiences of the late 1920's and early 1930's. The desire to prevent a recurrence of that upsurge in use of security credit was responsible for the enactment by Congress of the margin regulation provisions of the Securities Exchange Act in 1934.   *Pages 38 to 43*

Responsiveness to Credit Control

The safety and liquidity of security loans, willingness of borrowers to pay high rates of interest at times of rapidly rising security prices, and the emphasis placed by lenders on the value of collateral, rather than the borrower's ability to repay, have made security credit quite unresponsive to quantitative credit restriction at times. This has been particularly true on the occasions when economic conditions have been quite favorable to a long sustained rise in stock prices. These experiences have given rise to the adoption of selective credit controls.

Following a period of overexuberant expansion of security loans, a drastic contraction will inevitably follow when a major decline in security prices causes lenders to require additional collateral or a reduction of loans. At such times, security credit is quite unresponsive to efforts of the Federal Reserve System to expand borrowing to sustain the economy.

The case for selective control of security loans is thus based on the occasional need for such restraint to make general or quantitative credit control more effective. Selective control should not be justified by:

1. a dogmatic prejudice against the use of security credit;

2. the argument that such loans are not economically essential or that they divert credit from financing over-all business activity, or

3. the contention that security credit control can help stabilize the stock market and so contribute to business stability.

To prevent occasional excessive expansion and subsequent contraction of security credit that will undermine the effectiveness of over-all quantitative credit control, selective control of such credit on a *standby* basis should suffice. Control would then be applied by action of the regulatory authority only when a need is indicated. However, administrative difficulties arise in applying standby controls. These include not only questions of timing, but also the need of retraining the persons affected in complying with the regulations.

There are thus strong reasons for maintaining *continuous* selective regulation of security credit, with margin requirements set at moderate levels except on the occasions when an excessive or runaway rise in the volume of borrowing to purchase or carry securities is threatened. At such times, increases in margin requirements serve to limit the use of security credit.   *Pages 45 to 55*

Volume of Security Credit

Security credit can contribute to economic instability and lessen the effectiveness of over-all quantitative credit control only when its volume expands sharply and continuously, as it did in the late 1920's.

But that episode has not been repeated. Since 1930, security loans have constituted but a very small fraction of the nation's credit structure.

In the past two decades, security credit—both "wholesale" and "retail"—has averaged only a little more than 1% of private debt outstanding, except for a temporary bulge in the years 1944-46. Security loans have lagged far behind consumer and home mortgage loans in the post-World War II period. Except for the war years, brokers' loans amounted to as much as 1% of all business loans in only three out of the 21 years 1939-59, despite the fact that member banks possessed net free reserves and credit conditions were easy during much of this period.

During the 1950's, bank loans to purchase or carry securities have averaged only about 5% of all bank loans. Therefore, it has not been a rise in security loans, but rapid expansion of other classes of bank loans, that has been responsible for the adoption of restrictive general credit policies by the Federal Reserve System.   *Pages 56 to 68*

A ratio of customer security loans to the value of listed stocks, averaging around 2%, indicates that security credit has not significantly influenced the level of security prices in the past two decades. Changes in security credit outstanding do not appear to have been of sufficient magnitude to have had a significant influence on the fluctuations of stock prices.

The economic benefits of security credit, therefore, have been provided by a volume of loans that has not been large enough to affect either the stability of the economy or the effectiveness of quantitative credit control since the early 1930's.   *Pages 65 to 72*

Security Credit Regulation

The enactment of the margin regulation provisions of the Securities Exchange Act of 1934 followed a long period of study and debate of this issue.

Regulation of security credit was first suggested as a corrective for the money panics that occurred before the establishment of the Federal Reserve System, especially the panic of 1907. The New York Stock Exchange took the first step towards such regulation in 1913, when members were called upon to require "proper and adequate margin" in customer accounts. The Federal Reserve Act, enacted later that year, sought to make security loans less attractive to member banks by denying the rediscount privilege to such loans.

Stock market credit was regulated during World War I by a committee of bankers for the sole purpose of assuring that Treasury war financing would not be hampered by either a scarcity of funds for brokers' loans or an expansion of such credit. While this regulation was terminated soon after the end of the war, the experience demonstrated that selective control could be applied to security credit.   *Pages 75 to 79*

The great expansion of security credit during the 1920's, in the face of efforts by the Federal Reserve System to check it by general credit control measures and public warnings, produced a strong demand for regulation of security lending.

The Banking Act of 1933 gave the Federal Reserve Board new powers to limit the volume of security loans of member banks. But these controls over the *supply* of loanable funds have never been used because Congress proceeded to impose selective control over the *demand* for security loans through the margin provisions of the Securities Exchange Act of 1934.   *Pages 80 to 83*

Margin Provisions of the Securities Exchange Act

Intensive investigation and extended debate preceded enactment by Congress of the credit control provisions of the Securities Exchange Act of 1934.

A wide variety of proposals, ranging from outright prohibition of margin trading to special provisions to protect the small trader, were considered and rejected. The margin sections were rewritten repeatedly.

It can be concluded, therefore, that Sections 7 and 8 of the Securities Exchange Act of 1934 went as far as a critical Congress felt security credit regulation could be carried without injury to the economy.

The central feature of the margin sections of the law is its wide grant of authority to the Federal Reserve Board to set margin requirements for many, but by no means all, classes of loans to purchase or carry securities. By making the Board the administrative agency, Congress indicated its intent to make regulation of the *volume of security credit* the primary objective of margin regulation. Other objectives proposed at the time, such as protecting the small trader, limiting the volume of speculation or lessening fluctuations in stock

prices, were either made incidental to this primary
objective or ignored.   *Pages 85 to 96*

The Federal Reserve Regulations

Regulation T, first issued in 1934, and Regulation U, adopted in 1936, embody the basic policies
of Federal Reserve margin regulation. Regulation
T applies to brokers, and Regulation U to banks.

Most significant has been the limitation of Federal Reserve regulation to *initial* as distinct from
maintenance margin requirements. This recognized the fact that the chief objective of margin
regulation has been to limit the volume of credit
used for security speculation. By not requiring
that a specified margin be maintained at all times,
the Federal Reserve authorities have sought to
avoid forced selling from margin accounts when
the stock market declines. Such selling would contribute to instability of stock prices.

The Federal Reserve authorities have also
sought to lessen the effect of margin regulations
on the market's liquidity in two ways. Under
specified conditions, they have authorized security
substitutions in restricted accounts, and have permitted withdrawals of cash and securities when
securities are sold from such accounts.   *Pages 99 to 107*

Unregulated Security Loans

One problem that has proved difficult to resolve
has been the supervision of security collateral
loans said to be made for purposes other than the
purchase or carrying of securities—the "non-
purpose" loans. Wanting to hamper bank business
lending as little as possible, the Federal Reserve
authorities have been hesitant about policing "non-
purpose" loans under Regulation U, whereas they
require a signed affirmative declaration of pur-

pose from the brokerage house customer under Regulation T. Regulation U was amended in 1959, however, to require that a non-purpose statement must be signed both by the borrower and an officer of the lending bank.

The Board of Governors has not sought to extend margin regulation to lenders other than brokers, dealers and banks, although it required in 1960 that other persons extending credit on registered stocks in the ordinary course of business file reports on such loans.

The substantive provisions of Regulations T and U, apart from the initial margin percentages set, have reflected a consistent effort to use margin regulation primarily to limit the volume of credit used to purchase or carry securities. Examination of the historical record since 1934 suggests that the Board of Governors of the Federal Reserve System has also sought, where consistent with this objective, to lessen the impact of margin control upon the liquidity of the security markets, the raising of new capital through new issues of securities, and the use of security loans for business and consumption purposes. It has also shown an awareness of the danger that margin regulation may result merely in a shift of borrowing from brokerage house margin accounts to loans from banks or unregulated lenders.

However, experience has demonstrated that constant vigilance by the Board of Governors will be required if Regulations T and U are to be effective in regulating the total volume of security credit, rather than in merely diverting such borrowing from regulated to unregulated channels.   *Pages 107 to 112*

Effects of Changes in Margin Regulations

Increases in margin requirements have to date invariably slowed down or reversed a rising trend in customer net debit balances. Reductions in margin requirements have retarded or reversed a falling trend in debit balances.

Thus, margin controls have to date achieved the primary objective of limiting and regulating the volume of security credit.

The record also indicates that small increases in margin requirements have generally proved to be as effective as large increases in influencing the trend of customer borrowing.   *Pages 117 to 119*

On other scores, the statistical evidence of the effects of margin changes upon stock prices and the volume of turnover has been less conclusive. A majority of margin increases slowed down the stock market's price rise, but in no case halted or reversed the upward trend. A lowering of margin requirements was followed by a rise in stock prices or a slackening of the pace of a decline in each instance.

Trading volume has not been affected in any uniform manner by small margin increases, but has been reduced materially by each of the three increases of 25 percentage points.

During its first quarter century, margin regulation by the Board of Governors of the Federal Reserve System was conducted under economic conditions highly favorable to rising stock prices and a broadening of equity investment. Accelerated growth of the economy and a major inflation of the price level produced record corporate earnings and dividends. Common stock prices, as measured by the Standard and Poor's index of 500 issues, rose almost sixfold between 1934 and 1959.

A slackening of the rate of economic growth and a more stable trend of commodity prices could make the stock market much more sensitive to high margin requirements. Under such conditions, smaller changes in margin requirements than in the past would be preferable. The case for smaller changes is the stronger because small increases have hitherto proved as effective as large in halting a rise in customers' net debit balances—the chief objective of margin regulation.

Security credit can be regulated by changes in withdrawal and substitution provisions, as well as in initial margin requirements. Limitation on withdrawals of the proceeds of security sales from restricted accounts tends to reduce the volume of security credit in use. However, it also affects adversely the volume of trading and the liquidity of the market. A judicious combination of initial margin and retention requirement changes could make for more flexible, yet effective, security credit control—with lower initial margin requirements than would be called for if initial margin changes alone were used to regulate such credit.   *Pages 119 to 126*

Potential Dangers of Unregulated Lending

It is too early to reach final judgment as to the effects on the security markets and the economy of high margin requirements. The same can be said of the threat of a shift to unregulated forms and channels of borrowing on securities.

Many types of security loans are not subject to margin regulation. Under the statute, all borrowings on U. S. Government and state and local obligations and borrowings from banks on bonds other than convertible issues are exempt from margin restrictions. The law also exempts bank loans on unregistered securities for the purpose of purchasing or carrying any security other than listed stocks. Regulation U widens the area of exemption to bank loans on listed stocks made to buy or carry registered bonds and bank loans on convertible bonds.   *Pages 128 to 136*

Security loans from unregulated lenders such as factors and foreign banks are not affected by margin regulation. Another area not affected by regulation that is of substantial importance is the extension of credit that takes the form of re-purchase agreements rather than loans. Evasion of margin regulation can occur also through inade- quate policing of "non-purpose" loans.

The available evidence indicates that the vol- ume of unregulated lending to purchase or carry securities, although substantial in the aggregate, has hitherto not been large enough to undermine the effectiveness of over-all quantitative credit control or the stability of the security markets as a whole. But there is certainly no assurance that this will continue to be so in the future. In fact, episodes such as the widespread purchases of U. S. Government obligations on very thin or no mar- gins in 1958 have indicated that, when opportu- nities for profit are regarded as favorable, high margin requirements on listed stocks may be a factor in encouraging a large-scale shift of trading activity to exempted securities and heavy borrow- ing through unregulated channels.

The ever-present threat of evasion and large- scale avoidance is a most persuasive reason for moderation on the part of the Federal Reserve authorities in ordering margin increases and for prompt reductions to moderate margin require- ments when conditions permit. The alternative would be to proliferate new restrictions indefinitely to keep pace with new forms of evasion as they become known. To do this would require amend- ment of the law to give the Board of Governors the authority to regulate every type of security credit now known or that might hereafter be de- veloped, something the Board does not now pos- sess.

Pages 136 to 145

IN SUMMARY

Selective control of security credit by the Board of Governors of the Federal Reserve System has achieved its primary objectives during the quarter of a century since the Securities Exchange Act of 1934 was enacted.

On no occasion during this period has the volume of security credit expanded to an extent that has lessened the effectiveness of over-all quantitative credit control. Increases and decreases in security credit have not been large enough to affect materially the stability of the stock market.

To achieve its objectives, the Board of Governors of the Federal Reserve System has on occasion raised initial margin requirements to a very high level—to 100% in 1946 and to 90% in 1958. Margin requirements were 70% or higher during almost 11 of the 14 years following the end of World War II. They were 100% for a little over a year in 1946-47, and 90% in 1958-mid 1960.

Since economic conditions were highly favorable to the equity market throughout this period, high margin requirements did not have significant adverse consequences. Stock prices advanced to record levels, and the volume of trading expanded moderately in the years following World War II. Security credit, in its wholesale and retail uses, continued to perform functions of great value to the economy under these high margin requirements. However, such high margin requirements could well have serious adverse effects upon the breadth and the price level of the stock market under less favorable economic conditions which a slackening of the rate of growth of the economy and a stable or sagging commodity price level could bring about.

Under economic conditions less favorable to a broad rising market for stocks, experience indicates that changes in margin requirements could well be held within a narrower range. In the past quarter of a century, despite highly favorable stock market conditions, the volume of security credit was successfully controlled over extended periods with relatively small margin increases.

Questions for the Future

Four basic questions arise with regard to the future of margin regulations. These are:

1. Will the Federal Reserve authorities move promptly to minimize the restrictive effects of margin regulation upon the stock market when economic conditions become less favorable to equity investment and a broad demand for common stocks? And will authorities move promptly to increase the restrictive effect of margin regulation when conditions become favorable for a major and protracted rise in the stock market?

2. Can security credit perform the economic functions of facilitating the flow of capital into productive investment and of broadening the market for equities if initial margin requirements are kept above the 50% level when basic economic trends are less favorable to the equity markets?

3. Will growing resort to borrowing through unregulated channels at times of very high margin requirements cause an eventual breakdown of the effectiveness of security credit regulation?

4. Will the insight and experience gained through a quarter of a century of margin regulation lead to greater flexibility in the exercise of margin controls, with more sensitivity to changes in conditions affecting the security markets?

To guard against the dangers of harmful effects or a breakdown in effectiveness inherent in security credit regulation will require constant study of the effects of margin regulation by the Federal Reserve authorities, and the close cooperation of the financial community in bringing to the attention of the authorities pertinent developments as they appear.

SECTIONS 7 AND 8 OF THE SECURITIES EXCHANGE ACT OF 1934

Section 7—Margin Requirements

Sec. 7. (a) For the purpose of preventing the excessive use of credit for the purchase or carrying of securities, the Federal Reserve Board shall, prior to the effective date of this section and from time to time thereafter, prescribe rules and regulations with respect to the amount of credit that may be initially extended and subsequently maintained on any security (other than an exempted security) registered on a national securities exchange. For the initial extension of credit, such rules and regulations shall be based upon the following standard: An amount not greater than whichever is the higher of—

(1) 55 per centum of the current market price of the security, or

(2) 100 per centum of the lowest market price of the security during the preceding thirty-six calendar months, but not more than 75 per centum of the current market price.

Such rules and regulations may make appropriate provision with respect to the carrying of undermargined accounts for limited periods and under specified conditions; the withdrawal of funds or securities; the substitution or additional purchases of securities; the transfer of accounts from one lender to another; special or different transactions, and securities to which paragraph (2) of this subsection does not apply; the bases and the methods to be used in calculating loans, and margins and market prices; and similar administrative adjustments and details. For the purposes of paragraph (2) of this subsection, until July 1,

1936, the lowest price at which a security has sold on or after July 1, 1933, shall be considered as the lowest price at which such security has sold during the preceding thirty-six calendar months.

(b) Notwithstanding the provisions of subsection (a) of this section, the Federal Reserve Board, may, from time to time, with respect to all or specified securities or transactions, or classes of securities, or classes of transactions, by such rules and regulations (1) prescribe such lower margin requirements for the initial extension or maintenance of credit as it deems necessary or appropriate for the accommodation of commerce and industry, having due regard to the general credit situation of the country, and (2) prescribe such higher margin requirements for the initial extension or maintenance of credit as it may deem necessary or appropriate to prevent the excessive use of credit to finance transactions in securities.

(c) It shall be unlawful for any member of a national securities exchange or any broker or dealer who transacts a business in securities through the medium of any such member, directly or indirectly to extend or maintain credit or arrange for the extension or maintenance of credit to or for any customer—

(1) On any security (other than an exempted security) registered on a national securities exchange, in contravention of the rules and regulations which the Federal Reserve Board shall prescribe under subsections (a) and (b) of this section.

(2) Without collateral or on any collateral other than exempted securities and/or securities registered upon a national securities exchange, except in accordance with such rules and regulations as the Federal Reserve Board may prescribe (A) to permit under specified conditions and for a limited period any such member, broker, or dealer to maintain a credit initially extended in conformity with the rules and regulations of the Federal Reserve Board, and (B) to permit the extension or maintenance of credit in cases where the extension or maintenance of credit is not for the purpose of purchasing or carrying securities or of evading or circumventing the provisions of paragraph (1) of this subsection.

(d) It shall be unlawful for any person not subject to subsection (c) to extend or maintain credit or to arrange for the extension or maintenance of credit for the purpose of purchasing or carrying any security registered on a national securities exchange, in contravention of such rules and regulations as the Federal Reserve Board shall prescribe to prevent the excessive use of credit for the purchasing or carrying of or trading in securities in circumvention of the other provisions of this section. Such rules and regulations may impose upon all loans made for the purpose of purchasing or carrying securities registered on national securities exchanges limitations similar to those imposed upon members, brokers, or dealers by subsection (c) of this section and the rules and regulations thereunder. This subsection and the rules and regulations thereunder shall not apply (A) to a loan made by a person not in the ordinary course of his business, (B) to a loan on an exempted security, (C) to a loan to a dealer to aid in the financing of the distribution of securities to customers not through the medium of a national securities exchange, (D) to a loan by a bank on a security other than an equity security, or (E) to such other loans as the Federal Reserve Board shall, by such rules and regulations as it may deem necessary or appropriate in the public interest or for the protection of investors, exempt, either unconditionally or upon specified terms and conditions or for stated periods, from the operation of this subsection and the rules and regulations thereunder.

(e) The provisions of this section or the rules and regulations thereunder shall not apply on or before July 1, 1937, to any loan or extension of credit made prior to the enactment of this title or to the maintenance, renewal, or extension of any such loan or credit, except to the extent that the Federal Reserve Board may by rules and regulations prescribe as necessary to prevent the circumvention of the provisions of this section or the rules and regulations thereunder by means of withdrawals of funds or securities, substitutions of securities, or additional purchases or by any other device.

Section 8—Restrictions on Borrowing by Members, Brokers, and Dealers

Sec. 8. It shall be unlawful for any member of a national securities exchange, or any broker or dealer who transacts a business in securities through the medium of any such member, directly or indirectly—

(a) To borrow in the ordinary course of business as a broker or dealer on any security (other than an exempted security) registered on a national securities exchange except (1) from or through a member bank of the Federal Reserve System, (2) from any nonmember bank which shall have filed with the Federal Reserve Board an agreement, which is still in force and which is in the form prescribed by the Board, undertaking to comply with all provisions of this Act, the Federal Reserve Act, as amended, and the Banking Act of 1933, which are applicable to member banks and which relate to the use of credit to finance transactions in securities, and with such rules and regulations as may be prescribed pursuant to such provisions of law or for the purpose of preventing evasions thereof, or (3) in accordance with such rules and regulations as the Federal Reserve Board may prescribe to permit loans between such members and/or brokers and/or dealers, or to permit loans to meet emergency needs. Any such agreement filed with the Federal Reserve Board shall be subject to termination at any time by order of the Board, after appropriate notice and opportunity for hearing, because of any failure by such bank to comply with the provisions thereof or with such provisions of law or rules or regulations and, for any willful violation of such agreement, such bank shall be subject to the penalties provided for violations of rules and regulations prescribed under this title. The provisions of sections 21 and 25 of this title shall apply in the case of any such proceeding or order of the Federal Reserve Board in the same manner as such provisions apply in the case of proceedings and orders of the Commission.

(b) To permit in the ordinary course of business as a broker his aggregate indebtedness to all other persons, including customers' credit balances (but excluding indebtedness secured by exempted securities), to exceed such percentage of the net capital (exclusive of fixed assets and value of exchange membership) employed in the business, but not exceeding in any case 2,000 per centum, as the Commission may by rules and regulations prescribe as necessary or appropriate in the public interest or for the protection of investors.

(c) In contravention of such rules and regulations as the Commission shall prescribe for the protection of investors to hypothecate or arrange for the hypothecation of any securities carried for the account of any customer under circumstances (1) that will permit the commingling of his securities without his written consent with the securities of any other customer, (2) that will permit such securities to be commingled with the securities of any person other than a bona fide customer, or (3) that will permit such securities to be hypothecated, or subjected to any lien or claim of the pledge, for a sum in excess of the aggregate indebtedness of such customers in respect of such securities.

(d) To lend or arrange for the lending of any securities carried for the account of any customer without the written consent of such customer.

MAXIMUM LOAN VALUE OF SECURITIES UNDER REGULATION T, FOLLOWING EACH MARGIN CHANGE BY THE BOARD OF GOVERNORS OF THE FEDERAL RESERVE SYSTEM

Margin Requirement	*Maximum Loan Value*
Effective October 15, 1934: * the higher of (45% margin)	1. 55% of the current market price, or 2. 100% of the lowest market price of the security during preceding 36 calendar months, but not more than 75% of the current market price. No "short" margin
Effective February 1, 1936: the higher of (55% margin)	1. 45% of the current market price or 2. Same as 2 above. No "short" margin
Effective April 1, 1936: (55% margin)	Straight 45% for all securities No "short" margin
Effective November 1, 1937: (40% margin)	60% for all securities "long" 50% on "short" positions
Effective February 5, 1945: (50% margin)	50% for all securities "long"
Effective July 5, 1945: (75% margin)	25% for all securities "long" (specialist 50%) 75% on "short" positions
Effective January 21, 1946: (100% margin)	No loan value for securities "long" 100% on "short" positions

---

* The October 1 effective date in the Regulation was extended to October 15 by an exemption granted September 28.

Margin Requirement	Maximum Loan Value
Effective December 1, 1946: in subscription account (50% margin)	50% loan value for subscription to stocks by rights accruing to stockholder expiring in 90 days or less
Effective February 1, 1947: (75% margin)	25% for all securities "long" 75% on "short" positions
Effective March 30, 1949: (50% margin)	50% for all securities "long" 50% on "short" positions
Effective May 16, 1949: in subscription account (25% margin)	75% loan value on subscriptions by rights expiring within 90 days of issuance.
Effective July 20, 1949: in specialist account (no margin required)	good faith loan value. Can be 100% by mutual agreement.
Effective January 17, 1951: (75% margin)	25% for all securities "long" 75% on "short" positions
Effective February 20, 1953: (50% margin)	50% for all securities "long" 50% on "short" positions
Effective January 4, 1955: (60% margin)	40% for all securities "long" 60% on "short" positions
Effective April 23, 1955: (70% margin)	30% for all securities "long" 70% on "short" positions
Effective January 16, 1958: (50% margin)	50% for all securities "long" 50% on "short" positions
Effective August 5, 1958: (70% margin)	30% for all securities "long" 70% on "short" positions
Effective October 16, 1958: (90% margin)	10% for all securities "long" 90% on "short" positions
Effective June 15, 1959: (50% withdrawal)	10% for all securities "long" 90% on "short" positions (withdrawals) 50% "retention requirements"
Effective July 28, 1960: (70% margin)	30% for all securities "long" 70% on "short" positions (withdrawals) 50% "retention requirements"

Compiled by the New York Stock Exchange.

STATED REASONS FOR CHANGES IN MARGIN REQUIREMENTS BY THE BOARD OF GOVERNORS OF THE FEDERAL RESERVE SYSTEM

From 1934 through 1959, the Board of Governors of the Federal Reserve made 16 basic changes in margin requirements. In each case, the Board explained in its annual report the reasons for its action. The salient parts of these explanations, quoted from the Board's annual reports, are reproduced in this Appendix.

February 1, 1936—Upper limit of margin requirement raised from 45 to 55%

The 1936 Report stated: "The volume of credit extended . . . by member firms of the New York Stock Exchange who carry margin accounts, which began to increase about the middle of 1935, had increased since that time by about $213 million, or approximately 20 per cent. The borrowings of these firms at banks had increased by about $150 million, and bank loans on securities to borrowers other than brokers, after declining to September 1935, had subsequently shown a slight increase. . . . It appeared that, on the basis of past experience, a further advance in securities prices would be likely to be accompanied by a further growth in the use of credit in the stock market.

"The advance in stock prices, which began in March 1935 and continued until the middle of November, had been resumed during recent weeks . . . stock prices had risen to a . . . level . . . above that reached in November and above the level of 1926. At the same time the volume of trading had increased again to about 3 million shares per day.

169

"While the existing amount of borrowing was low as compared with some past years, it was at about the level from which the great increase that accompanied the stock market boom of the 1920's commenced, and it was believed that the restraining influence of any increase in margin requirements, in order to be effective in forestalling an excessive growth in the use of credit for the purpose of purchasing or carrying securities . . . should be applied before an unhealthy development of credit . . . gets underway.

"In addition, there continued to exist a large volume of excess reserves of member banks, amounting to over $3 billion, which might be drawn upon in part to finance operations in the securities markets."

April 1, 1936—Uniform margin requirement established at 55%

"The Board adopted . . . a margin formula based on a percentage of the current market value for the reason that such a formula is the simplest, most easily understood, and the most commonly used by banks in determining margin requirements on security loans.

"The statutory formula, stated . . . in the Securities Exchange Act of 1934, would be burdensome for most banks since few banks have a large volume of security loans and most of them are not under the necessity of being familiar with market quotations or the details of the securities loan business . . .

"Furthermore, it was agreed that in Regulation U a loan value should be given to unregistered stocks. The use of the statutory formula as a basis for fixing the loan value of an unregistered stock would be impracticable as would any other formula based in whole or in part on the lowest value of an unregistered stock during an antecedent period, and it would be undesirable to have the loan value of unregistered stocks fixed on a different basis from that of registered stocks.

"It was also agreed . . . that the principal purpose underlying the statutory formula when the Securities Exchange Act of 1934 was passed had been largely accomplished in that margin

requirements, which were very low when the formula first became effective, had increased automatically under the formula
to a much higher average level; and that a margin requirement
based on a flat percentage of the current market price, if the
margin requirement were sufficiently high, could be justified in
existing circumstances on the ground that a large majority of
stocks listed on national securities exchanges had increased to a
point where they were no longer subject to the antipyramiding
restrictions contained in the statutory formula."

November 1, 1937—Margin requirement decreased to 40%

"It was apparent that the progress of economic recovery was
suffering an interruption.

"Security offerings in the third quarter of 1937 were the small-
est since the revival of activity in the capital markets in the
early part of 1935. . . .

"Prices of both securities and commodities had declined sharply.

"Productive activity following a year of output at the highest
levels since 1929 declined in September and October. . . . The
construction industry had experienced a disappointing year.

"Since September 1 there had been a decline in the loans of
reporting member banks to brokers and dealers of $440 million,
the largest decline since 1931, and such loans had reached the
lowest level in 2 years. Credit extended by brokers to their
customers had declined over 20 per cent, . . . to a point approximately $100 million below the level at the time the present
margin requirements were established. . . ."

February 5, 1945—Margin requirement increased to 50%

". . . the history of the Securities Exchange Act of 1934 shows
that action by the Board on margin requirements should take
into account the amount of credit outstanding and also the level
of stock prices, the general business situation and related factors;

". . . the general level of stock-market prices during recent
weeks had been rising to a succession of new 7-year highs, the
volume of trading being above normal;

". . . the volume of stock-market credit (as measured by customers' debit balances) had been increasing and was for the first time above any level since the beginning of 1938;

". . . the proportion of margin trading by the public commonly rises in sharp advances in the market, and along with the increase in the proportion of such trading there had been an increase also in the number of shares being carried in margin accounts."

July 5, 1945—Margin requirement increased to 75%

". . . the Board considered that the continued upward trend and increased activity in the securities markets justified the action for the purpose of preventing the excessive use of credit for purchasing or carrying securities.

"In addition, account was taken of the fact that the amount of credit used for these purposes, after decreasing in March, had increased again thereafter by a substantial amount.

"All of these considerations were deemed by the Board to have special weight by reason of the existence of an unprecedented and growing volume of purchasing power in the hands of individuals and corporations, as a result of war and war financing, at a time when there was an acute shortage of goods, and the consequent danger of general inflation."

January 21, 1946—Margin requirement increased to 100%

"During the period of reconversion from a wartime to a peacetime economy, the country was being exposed to powerful inflationary pressures. . . .

"This period had also been characterized by public pressure for premature removal of governmental wartime controls, with the consequent effect of promoting speculative activity.

"Restriction of the use of credit in the securities market would tend to discourage speculative activity which was both a characteristic and a feeder of inflation. In these circumstances, any expansion in the use of credit for the purpose of buying or trading in registered securities was, in the judgment of the Board, an excessive use of credit and consequently should be prevented under the legislative mandate to the Board.

"While the Board recognized that action in this field could have only a limited effect in combating general inflation, it believed that this action was not only in accordance with its legal obligations, but would help, though to a necessarily limited extent, to protect the national economy from the dangers of inflation."

February 1, 1947—Margin requirement decreased to 75%

"In the [last] year . . . economic conditions and prospects had altered somewhat. The supply of money was reduced during the year as a result of a substantial decrease of the Government debt held by the banking system, and this had had a salutary effect.

"In contrast with the behavior of most prices, stock prices, which had risen sharply for several months prior to January 1946 and continued to rise somewhat further after that time, subsequently declined materially. . . .

"At the same time, the volume of credit in the stock market had been substantially reduced until that used for carrying listed securities was at about the lowest level in the last 30 years."

March 30, 1949—Margin requirement decreased to 50%

". . . there were increasing evidences that inflationary pressures were subsiding and that a readjustment from a highly inflationary situation was taking place. It was the view of the Board that, in these conditions, the time had arrived when action to reduce margin requirements should be taken."

January 17, 1951—Margin requirement increased to 75%

"Although the total amount of credit in use in the stock market had not assumed heavy proportions, there had been some increase during the preceding several months, together with increases in the volume of trading and in prices of securities. The expanding business and economic situation appeared to be encouraging stock market activity and speculation, and the Board of Governors believed that in the existing circumstances a further substantial price advance supported by a rapid expansion of stock market credit was a distinct possibility. The increase in margin requirements was effected as a preventive measure and as a supplement to the steps previously taken in the credit and monetary area to lessen inflationary pressures."

February 20, 1953—Margin requirement decreased to 50%

". . . by February 1953 inflationary pressures had moderated and, with the margin requirements fixed at 75 per cent, there had been no substantial increase in the total amount of credit in use in the stock market. Accordingly, the Board concluded that margin requirements of 50 per cent would be adequate to prevent the excessive use of credit for the purchasing and carrying of securities and that a reduction to that level would be in harmony with the System's overall credit and monetary policy under current conditions."

January 4, 1955—Margin requirement increased to 60%

"During the latter part of 1954, the economy began a recovery from the recession that prevailed during the latter part of 1953 and the first part of 1954. The upturn was accompanied by a marked increase in stock market activity. . . . Stock market credit had risen substantially from early 1954. . . . This occurred during a period in which the volume of trading on securities exchanges had reached the highest levels in several years and evidences of substantial speculative activity were appearing.

"The Board's action in increasing margin requirements was designed to prevent the recovery from being hampered by excessive speculative activity in the stock markets."

April 23, 1955—Margin requirement increased to 70%.

"The period following the increase in margin requirements in January 1955 was marked by further growth, although at a somewhat lesser rate, in the volume of credit extended . . . for the purchase and carrying of securities, and by further indications of expanding speculative activity. This second action to increase margin requirements . . . was designed as an additional step to prevent excessive use of credit from adding to . . . [speculative] pressures."

January 16, 1958—Margin requirement decreased to 50%.

"For several months . . . common stock prices had been moving within a narrow range at a level approximately one-sixth below the peak reached in July 1957, and at this lower range the yields on stocks were restored to a point above those available on high-grade corporate bonds. The price movement was accompanied by a substantial reduction in stock market credit outstanding which, at the end of 1957, was estimated at about $3.6 billion. . . . With the downward trend of general economic developments . . . . stock market behavior reflected a psychology of caution.

"Although the historical record suggested the probability of some increase in customer debit balances following a margin reduction, it did not appear that such action at this time would be any great stimulant to stock market activity. Instead, the reaction of investors seemed likely to depend largely on their appraisal of the over-all economic situation.

"In these circumstances, a 70 per cent margin requirement could no longer be justified on the grounds . . . [of] potential excessive speculative activity and potential undue use of credit to finance such activity."

August 5, 1958—Margin requirement increased to 70%

"By this date there was clear statistical evidence that recovery in economic activity and production had gained considerable momentum and was likely to go forward. The recovery was accompanied by a rise in stock prices sufficient to carry common stock yields below yields on bonds of the same companies, and by a sharp increase in the volume of stock market credit which by July had reached a level some 20 per cent higher than at the beginning of the year. In view of this rapid rise in credit and the re-emergence of an investment psychology favoring the purchase of stocks as a hedge against potential inflation, which would be a particular inducement to borrowing for the purpose, the margin requirements were restored to the 70 per cent level."

October 16, 1958—Margin requirement increased to 90%

"Following the increase in margin requirements . . . early in August, common stock prices continued their upward climb in a heavy volume of trading activity. . . . By October this price movement had carried common stock yields to a level more than half a percentage point below the average yield on high-grade corporate bonds. After a pause in August, stock market credit likewise resumed its upward thrust and latest estimates placed the volume of total customer credit at above $4.3 billion. In addition, the number of open margin accounts was reported to have increased considerably from June to September.

"Prevalent psychology, favoring equities, including those of a speculative character, as a medium of investment in preference to fixed-income obligations, appeared to reflect not only growing public confidence in continued business improvement but apprehension as to an intensification of inflationary pressures. In light of the developments in the market, the margin requirements were increased to 90 per cent . . . with a view to preventing the excessive use of credit for purchasing or carrying registered stocks."

Governor Robertson voted against this action for the following reasons:

"(1) Under withdrawal and substitution rules in effect at that time, a customer selling securities in a margin account was free to purchase an equal market value of securities or to withdraw the margin currently required on such a purchase. Thus, if he sold $1,000 of securities, he could replace them with a $1,000 purchase of securities, or he could withdraw $700 in cash under a 70 per cent margin requirement or $900 under a 90 per cent margin requirement. Consequently, Governor Robertson felt, the increased margin requirements would apply in practice only to new extensions of credit and not to the turnover of credit already in the market. It would fail, he believed, to reach the most important aspect at that time of the 'excessive use of credit' and would therefore be a relatively futile and ineffective action, the psychological effect of which might be the reverse of that intended.

"(2) Also because of the then existing withdrawal and substitution rules, the increased margin requirements would justifiably enlarge the inequity as between customers who could continue to trade on lower margins and new customers who could be subject to higher margins.

"(3) The higher margin requirements, coupled with the existing withdrawal and substitution rules, would tend to encourage a weakening of margin accounts and create dangers of cumulative forced selling in undermargined accounts if stock prices should fall."

May 1, 1959—Regulations T and U amended in order further to restrict withdrawals of cash or securities from so-called "restricted accounts."

"The purpose of these amendments was to make the Regulation(s) more effective in . . . preventing the excessive use of credit for purchasing or carrying securities."

Background:

For background on the operation of the security markets and security credit, see H. Parker Willis and Jules I. Bogen, *Investment Banking* (New York: Harper & Brothers, 1936); Bartow Griffiss, *The New York Call Money Market* (New York: The Ronald Press Company, 1925); C. A. Dice and W. J. Eiteman, *The Stock Market* (New York: McGraw-Hill Book Co., 1941); George F. Leffler, *The Stock Market* (New York: The Ronald Press Company, 1957).

Economic Impact of Security Credit:

For the most thorough discussion of the economic theory aspects of security credit, consult Fritz Machlup, *The Stock Market, Credit, and Capital Formation* (London: William Hodge and Company, Limited, 1940). An exhaustive treatment of the whole subject of security credit is contained in Twentieth Century Fund, *The Security Markets* (New York: The Twentieth Century Fund, 1935). See also L. H. Haney, L. S. Logan, and H. S. Gravens, *Brokers' Loans: A Study in the Relation Between Speculative Credits and the Stock Market, Business, and Banking* (New York: Harper & Brothers, 1932); J. A. Ross, *Speculation, Stock Prices, and Industrial Fluctuations* (New York: Ronald Press, 1938).

On the Magnitude of Security Credit:

The New York Stock Exchange has compiled the best set of statistics on member firm borrowings. See also *Federal Reserve Bulletin*. For historical statistics on *the total* magnitude of se-

178

curity credit, see: U. S. Congress, Senate Committee on Banking and Currency, "Operation of the National and Federal Reserve Banking Systems," Hearings before a subcommittee, Part VII, Appendix, 71st Congress, 1931; Benjamin Beckhart, *The New York Money Market* (New York: Columbia University Press, 1932), Vol. III. Also see above: Haney, *Brokers' Loans*, Machlup, *The Stock Market* and Twentieth Century Fund, *The Security Markets*.

History of Security Credit:

On the early use of security credit in Europe, consult: R. D. Richards, *The Early History of Banking in England* (London: Staples Press, Limited, 1929) and Ellis T. Powell, *The Evolution of the Money Market* (London: The Financial News, 1915). By far the best history of the development of security credit in the United States is Margaret G. Myers, *The New York Money Market* (New York: Columbia University Press, 1931), Vol. I. A detailed, valuable, and interesting account of the early development in the United States appears in Joseph S. Davis, *Essays in the Earlier History of American Corporations* (Cambridge: Harvard University Press, 1917). N. S. B. Gras, *The Massachusetts First National Bank of Boston, 1784-1934* (Cambridge: Harvard University Press, 1937) contains considerable detail, including rates on early security loans. Oliver M. W. Sprague's well known *History of Crises Under the National Banking System* (Washington: Government Printing Office, 1910) contains an analysis of the operation of security credit in the "money panics" that occurred before the Federal Reserve System.

Early Attempts to Regulate Security Credit:

See above Twentieth Century Fund, *The Security Markets* and, below, Robert E. Harris, *Federal Margin Requirements*. See also State of New York, *Report of Governor Hughes Committee on Speculation in Securities and Commodities*, 1909; H. G. S. Noble, *The New York Stock Exchange in the Crisis of 1914* (New York: Country Life Press, 1915); Lester Chandler, *Benjamin*

Strong, Central Banker (Washington: The Brookings Institution, 1958); Seymour E. Harris, *Twenty Years of Federal Reserve Policy* (Cambridge: Harvard University Press, 1933), and the following publications of U. S. Congress, Senate Committee on Banking and Currency: "Regulation of the Stock Exchange," Hearings, 63rd Congress, 1913; Senate Report, No. 133, 1913; "Brokers' Loans," Senate Report, No. 1124, 70th Congress, 1928; "Prohibiting Trading on Margins on the New York Stock Exchange," Hearings, 71st Congress, 1931.

The Legislative History and Operation of the Securities Exchange Act:

For the legislative history of the Securities Exchange Act, the indispensable source is of course the hearings and report of the so-called Pecora Committee: Senate Committee on Banking and Currency, "Stock Exchange Practices," Hearings, Part 15 and Senate Report, No. 1455, 73rd Congress, 1934. See also House Committee on Interstate and Foreign Commerce, "Stock Exchange Regulation," Report No. 1383 and No. 1838, 73rd Congress, 1934. Charles H. Meyer, *The Securities Exchange Act of 1934, Analyzed and Explained* (New York: Francis Emory Fitch, Inc., 1934) did just what its title suggested.

On the operation of the Act, the *Federal Reserve Bulletin* contains the rules and regulations, and interpretations under which the control of security credit has been administered. The most exhaustive single study is that of Robert E. Harris, *Federal Margin Requirements: A Selective Instrument of Monetary Policy* (an unpublished Ph.D. dissertation in the Library of the University of Pennsylvania, 1958). Kemper Simpson, *The Margin Trader* (New York: Harper & Brothers, 1938) is sharply critical of the Securities and Exchange Commission, security credit control, and margin trading in general.

Very valuable are the hearings and reports of the Fulbright Committee: Senate Committee on Banking and Currency, "Stock Market Study," Hearings, 84th Congress, 1955; Senate Report No. 375, 1955; and "Factors Affecting the Stock Market," Staff Report, 84th Congress, 1955.

INDEX

Acceptances, bankers', 51
Accounts:
  restricted, 125-126
    substitutions and withdrawals, 101, 104-107
  subscription, 108
Adjusted debit balance, 104-105
Agricultural loans, 51
American stock exchange, 131
  daily cash settlements, 4
Anderson, Robert B., Secretary of the Treasury, 131
Anti-pyramiding effects, contraction of security loans, 43
Association of Stock Exchange Firms, 109
Auction markets, 20

Balances:
  adjusted debit, 104-105
  cash, of member firms, carrying margin accounts, 38 (chart), 40
  customers' net debit, 70, 99, 105n, 118-119
  debit, 60, 64, 69n
    adjusted, 104-105
    net, 105n
Bankers' acceptances, 51
Banking Act of 1933, 81-83, 86, 92
  prohibits member hands to act as agents for nonbanking lenders, 83, 84
  provisions, 81-83, 154
  regulates volume of bank security lending, 82-83

Banks and banking:
  borrowing from banks on bonds and unlisted stocks, 133-136
  brokers' loans, 11
  call loans, amount of, 3
  commercial:
    favor business borrowers, 32, 33
    security loans in portfolios of, 31-33
    security loans made by, 29
  Congressional investigation, 81
  interbank deposits, 6
  margin requirements on Government securities, 132
  out-of-towns, source of security loans, 3, 4
  personal loans, 141
  savings, security loans by, 3
  security loans
    1881-1920 (chart), 5
    1939-59, 57-60; (tables), 58-60
    action required to bring excepted loans under regulation, 136
    Federal Reserve regulations, 13-14
    "non-purpose" loans, 136-138
    ratio to total bank loans, 1926-59 (chart), 68
    reports to Federal Reserve, 14, 77-78
    to purchase bonds and unregistered stock, 135